MATTHEW OF VENDÔME

ARS VERSIFICATORIA

(The Art of the Versemaker)

MEDIAEVAL PHILOSOPHICAL TEXTS IN TRANSLATION
No. 22

James H. Robb, L.S.M., Ph.D., Editor

MATTHEW OF VENDÔME

ARS VERSIFICATORIA

(The Art of the Versemaker)

Translated from the Latin
With an Introduction

By

ROGER P. PARR

Associate Professor of Classical and Medieval Rhetoric
Marquette University

MARQUETTE UNIVERSITY PRESS
MILWAUKEE, WISCONSIN
1981

Library of Congress Catalogue Card Number: 80-84768
© Copyright, 1981, The Marquette University Press
Milwaukee, Wisconsin
Printed in the United States of America
ISBN 0-87462-222-0

Mariae

[CONTENTS]

PREFACE

This translation of Matthew of Vendôme's *Ars Versificatoria* is based on the text printed by Edmond Faral in *Les Arts Poétiques du XIIe et du XIIIe Siècle,* published in 1924 by Librairie Ancienne Honore Champion and reprinted in 1971.

There exists at least four major manuscripts of the *Ars Versificatoria.* The one printed by Faral is that of Glasgow in the Hunterian Museum, numbered 511. Other manuscripts in England are in Balliol library, Oxford: one is numbered 263, folio 138-53; the other is numbered 276, folio 108-27. The latter, erroneously attributed to Gervais de Melkley, is missing the concluding thirty-four line verse epilogue. The Palatine Library of Vienna holds the fourth manuscript. Part one is numbered 246, folio 45^b -50^b and part two, folio 65^a - 68^b.

No definitive Latin text exists. Though a comparative analysis reveals differences in language varients and in minor details of matter, the Glasgow manuscript printed by Faral presents the essential doctrine and is, of course, more readily available for reference. For the convenience of reference I have retained the organization and paragraph numbering which Faral has imposed upon the text and have placed all source references in footnotes. In order to provide the reader with some sense of the nature of the medieval manuscript I have translated the rubrics and replaced them within the text in bold face type. The outline headings inclosed in brackets are not part of the text; they follow the designations of content set by Faral.

So as not to "play traitor to the text" I have tended toward a fairly literal translation with emphasis on exact meaning with some preservation of the flow of the Latin word. I have, therefore, retained a certain dedication to the etymology of words and have tried to draw some tone or color from it when choosing the English words in translation. Whenever possible I have attempted to retain any creative, symbolic or figurative aspects of language which reveal the individuality of the author and the flavor of his time. Thus, for instance, I translate *Set quia stipulationis neverca est dilatio:* "Because delay is the stepmother of covenant," when it might read "Because delay is the enemy of a promise given." Again, I retain Tullius since it indicates Cicero's name commonly used in the Middle Ages. My aim is to reveal as accurately as possible the author: his own questionable language skill and his attitude toward rhetorical practice, as well as his personality; all are consistently revealed in his text.

Of the standard treatises of *Artes Poeticae,* Matthew's style is particularly labored. There seems little doubt that this work is a teacher's manual when one notes the numerous instances in which the student is referred to as "listener." The "monotonous uniformity" indicated by Sedgwick can be explained perhaps in part by the fact the Matthew was writing a manual primarily for his own use. For this reason I have studiously avoided changing a word or expression for the purpose of variety or "cleaning up the text." The original is considerably dull and repetitious, with its only relief being the scathing attacks on his enemy, Arnulf, referred to as Rufus. He appears feverishly intent on persuading the youthful students of the foul nature of his rival.

To further maintain the full nature of the complete original text I have translated Matthew's lengthy listing of adjectives and verbs in toto. I have as far as possible endeavored to maintain also the general visual effect of the Faral text. Though it is impossible to provide the Latin hexameter form of Matthew's illustrative examples, I have retained somewhat the visual line form in order to suggest the image of verse.

It is clear that the student handbooks of the time were exercise manuals based on the detailed study of standard classical writers, of whom only a few were first rate Latinists. The rebirth of Latin studies early in the twelfth century prompted such handbooks designed to demonstrate the means of developing a traditional idea with rhetorical variety and skill. The primary motive was to revive and cleanse the Latin language. There is no attempt to discuss aesthetics or set forth a theory of style. The emphasis is on form, and rhetorical ingenuity substituted for originality and imagination.

I wish to thank Richard E. Arnold, S.J. and James H. Robb to whom I am indebted for their generous aid in numerous textual difficulties.

INTRODUCTION

Man is a speaking animal because he is a social animal. Since communication is vital to his effective development, it is not difficult to comprehend
the fundamental and pervasive role of the language arts in man's history.
Nor is it surprising that so many of the illustrious men who have contributed significantly to the illumination and definition of the continuous
achievements of civilization were themselves directly involved with the arts
of discourse in theory as well as practice. Rhetoric formed the basis of
education; in critical analysis, whether one scrutinized the work of the
orator-statesman, the historian or the poet, the art of rhetoric provided the
structured guide.[1]

Though the arts of discourse have been designated by the general rubric
"rhetoric," a comprehensive view discloses that a variety of titles have been
employed to signify the evolution of the systematized corpus of language
rules and expressive techniques. For the most part the prescriptions have
been assigned a title indicating a prevailing expressive mode of the time.
The conscious precision detailing the techniques by which ideas are effectively communicated reveals the habit of rigid self-analysis characteristic of
the history of philosophic thought.

Nor has the focus on human language waned. The floodgate widens,
rather, as one witnesses again a continually swelling tide. The flow is enormous. One might say that communications dominate our age with perhaps
an even greater consciousness of its saturating and vital importance. More
than ever it appears that man's social effectiveness is commensurate with his
knowledge of language and his expressive skill. A veritable encyclopedia of
titles indicates the range and the depth of language studies: semantics,
semiology, cybernetics, inter and intra-personal communication, organiza-
tional comunication, rhetoric of politics, the great variety of ethnic
rhetorics, only begin the list. Once more significant philosophical attentions
are centering on the nature of the word as effectively representing reality.
The problem of *verbum et veritas* haunts us still.

---

[1] D. L. Clark, *Rhetoric in Greco-Roman Education* (New York, 1957).

The most significant of contemporary studies attempt to gather the vast accumulative experience and thought concerning man's existence, thus placing considerable emphasis on symbol and myth as well as the combined effect of all sign systems.[2] On the surface the flood of works investigating communication by means other than words reflects the age of technology and the resulting interest in oral and visual image. This re-emphasis on oral communication recalls the role of oratory in the classical world which developed the term "rhetoric." Subsequent literary convergence was mirrored in the titles *On Composition, On the Sublime, On Style, On Orthography, On the Art of Grammar.*

CLASSICAL INFLUENCE ON THE MEDIEVAL ARTS OF DISCOURSE

In the early Christian world oratory served the church as formerly it had served the state, and thus *Ars Praedicandi* eventually came to indicate specific language prescriptions.[3] It was eventually the pragmatic and sophistic tradition which contributed most to the preservation of that matter and subsequently formed the *Artes Poeticae.* Once again a crisis in speculative thought brought about this substitute for a philosophic view, found not in the broad field of literature and philosophy, but in the study of rhetoric alone, with emphasis on form and style rather than on originality of idea. This loss of the philosophic view of language and literature brought about the disappearance of the essential difference between rhetoric and poetic. Therefore what survived through the post-classical rhetoricians and grammarians were those doctrines and rules of language which, when woven into an elaborate system of devices and techniques, became so organized and structured as to render them easily accessible for a variety of uses. Purpose, organization and emphasis of matter changed as society evolved and changed, providing new uses for old and standard material. *Grammatica* served effectively the speaking and writing arts. *Dialectica* was the philosopher's tool and *disputatio* trained the university student in the art of reasoning. Political oratory, homeletic, literature, philosophy, diplomacy, civil law, ecclesiastical law were all served by systematized language techniques.

By the eleventh century the flowering of the language arts is reflected in the diversity of manual titles: *Ars Praedicandi* (thematic sermon), *Ars Dictaminis* (letter writing), *Ars Rithmica* (rhythmic composition), *Ars Notaria* (legal documentation), *Ars Disputatio* (argumentation), *Rhetorica Ecclesiastica*

---

[2] This new philosophic investigation of the unified significance of all sign systems forms the comparatively new study semiology. See Roland Barthes, *Éléments de Sémiologie,* (1964, Editions du Seuil, Paris).

[3] St. Augustine's influence on the move from paganism to Christianity cannot be overemphasized. His *De Doctrina Christiana* reveals his efforts in bringing about this difficult transition: see also Joseph Finaert, *Saint Augustin Rhéteur* (Paris, 1939) and Henri Marrou, *Saint Augustine and His Influence through the Ages,* trans. Patrick Hepburne-Scott (New York, 1957).

(church rhetoric), *De Schematibus et Tropis* (figures and tropes), *Ars Metrica, Ars Poetria, Ars Versificatoria* (versification). The flood of handbooks indicates clearly the pragmatic exploitation of the devices of style of classical rhetoric.[4] Significant treatments of literary or poetic theory as such are rare. The *Ars Versificatoria* translated in this volume is an example of the practical service rendered by adapting the common doctrine of language form and techniques to a particular communication mode.

The Vernacular Tradition Versus the "New Poetry"

Despite the strengthening vernacular literary tradition and the general withering of the Latin language, a metrical Latin poetry continued under the auspices of monasticism, first in Germany and later in Northern France. Influence from the changing social and political scene is reflected in the predominantly national and religious themes. The Latin verse which appeared was somewhat crude but energetic and forceful. In the twelfth century, however, a new Latin verse developed; its themes and style were rigorously classical.[5] Attempts to purify Latin by replacing barbarisms with rhetorical ornament and versification produced a writing elegant in form but sterile. The tiresome overuse of remote themes recast into this "new poetry" with flagrant lack of originality and feeling produced an array of rhetorical mosaics only. The new poetry was at first almost exclusively elegiac. It was wrought according to rule. Man during this period was conditioned by doctrine in every sphere, and contemporary poetic doctrine said little concerning inspiration or perceptive insight. It said perfect the rule as moral doctrine said perfect your life. In both spheres this meant attempting to overcome the human disposition to defect and error.

The vogue for verse and the use of metrical form prompted the literary prescriptions of the twelfth and thirteenth centuries. These were the works Chaucer so effectively satirized.[6] His view is without doubt a perceptive one. A considerable variety of evidence and individual judgment throws light on the exact nature of these manuals. Poetic handbooks, grammars, as well as works of philosophy, history and science were composed in metrical form. Elegance and superior literary skill were associated with verse. Thus it became the common communication mode. Even letters and sermons were part of this tradition.

Medieval poetry was typical and it was idealized. The revival of interest in Latin verse provided the ideal. The making of verse in the twelfth and thirteenth centuries particularly, was a process of fitting the ideal into proper form, and the form like the matter idealized became fixed. The aim was

---

[4] In Aristotle's *Rhetoric* the discussion of style is contained in the third and shortest of its three books. His primary concern is the reasoning process as basic persuasion.

[5] See W. B. Sedgwick, "The Style and Vocabulary of the Latin Arts of Poetry of the Twelfth and Thirteenth Centuries," *Speculum* 3, pp. 349-381.

[6] See *Nun's Priest's Tale*, 11. 527 ff.

formal perfection through the techniques of language, and the work of the versifier was judged according to the perfection of that form. Because form fell within the conscious control of the writer, the craft of medieval verse could be taught and learned. Literary art was practiced by conscious imitation of Latin models and by studiously avoiding defects of form and style. Most treatises contain sections listing the defects to be avoided.[7]

It was not until these prescriptions for the writing of Latin verse were adapted to verse writing in the vernacular that a poetry of feeling and stimulation developed. The choice of original and varied subjects and the subtlety and flexibility of a language in the very process of finding its identity contributed enormously to a poetry of original perception and charm. Even in the vernacular, however, one observes that distinguished poetic achievement is commensurate with fresh and original poetic vision. The *Roman de la Rose* dulls considerably in the shadow of the *Divine comedy* and the *Canterbury Tales*.

The Survival of Classical Texts

Our view of the kind of emphasis given to expressive techniques is seen primarily through the prescriptive handbooks which have come down to us, and of course, in the surviving evidence which its practice provides. Such evidence can, however, be somewhat misleading for numerous reasons, one of which is the clarity and accuracy of manuscripts. Thus the circumstances which produced them and the condition of their survival ought to be assessed. Vital, too, is the accumulation of comment and reference by perceptive commentators both of the time and of succeeding ages. Such comment, of course, must be considered in light of its personal, political and literary context.

Early centers important in the survival of classical texts were Monte Cassino founded by St. Benedict in 529 and the great library established by Cassiodorus. As minister to Theodoric he was able to indulge his love of learning, and he is responsible for a great portion of the corpus of classical learning known today.[8]

General learning had come to a virtual standstill on the continent as a result of the Barbaric invasion when scholars abruptly dispossessed fled in panic across the sea presumably carrying many precious volumns with them. In the ascendancy of the vernacular tongues was laid the foundation of future nations. Consequent to the rise of political and national interests and the hostility of the Church, classical learning was shamefully neglected, even forbidden. Consequently the growth of vernacular languages contributed to an early decay of Latin. Because of universal pronunciation difficulties barbarous spellings flourished; grammar rules and metrics were ignored or abandoned.

---

[7] See *Ars Versificatoria* I, 30 ff and IV 25 ff.

[8] A. C. Clark, "The Reappearance of the Texts of the Classics," *Transactions of the Bibliographical Society*, 2nd Series, Vol. II (London, 1922).

But classical learning managed to survive, and a major force in that process stemmed from the Irish missionaries' eagerness for travel. Their monasteries established at Iona, Lindesfarne, Babbio and St. Gall became quiet repositories of numerous manuscripts. However, at Parma in 780 a famous meeting occurred which affected the entire culture of the West. Charlemagne, distressed at the decline of culture in Gall and elsewhere persuaded Alcuin to help him with his plan for a general intellectual revival based primarily on skill in expression. Thus Alcuin whose own interests focused on rhetoric, orthography and grammar, and responsible for the fame of the Cathedral School of York with a library said to surpass any of its time, was a major force in shaping the general character of medieval education.[9] Though national cultures were forming at this time, Alcuin remained completely in the Latin tradition and is one of the chief conveyers of ancient learning to the later Middle Ages. He removed his monks from the vineyard and trained them as scribes for the more important work of copying manuscripts. The education plan envisioned by Charlemagne was continued by his successors.

The process of linguistic decay was slowed, then, as classical Latin was re-vitalized and trained scribes produced more accurate manuscripts. The plan initiated by Alcuin was extended to monasteries at Fulda, Lorsch, Cologne, Corvei, Ferriers, Corbie, with others at York, Tours and Rome; they were mainly responsible for the survival of classical texts. Monasteries and cathedral libraries gathered enormous holdings as manuscripts were exchanged and copies ordered by alert abbots who sent scholars or agents from library to library collecting and reproducing. The traffic must have been considerable if one is to judge by the number of manuscripts and letters which have survived. This traffic also accounts for much of the transmission of textual error, confusion of colophon, faulty attribution of authorship and source, and of inaccuracies and confusion resulting from numerous scribal differences and defficiencies.

The nature of the incredible survival of classical manuscripts is revealed in part by the story of the vigorous search instigated centuries later by the rise of humanism in Italy and elsewhere.[10] As Alcuin directed the general course of medieval learning, so Petrarch influenced the Renaissance. Convinced that classical writings contained the summit of wisdom and right conduct, he fixed his attention on Cicero and never abandoned his search for new texts. His collection of manuscripts was extensive and with his friend Boccaccio sparked great interest in the search for manuscripts.

The most colorful and revealing examples of the feverish search is that conducted by Niccolo Niccoli. The narrative of his large scale research organization illustrates a process which had begun much earlier. It throws light, too, on the practices and conditions responsible for the survival of

---

[9] See W. Howell, ed. and trans. *The Rhetoric of Alcuin and* Charlemagne (Princeton, 1941); L. Wallach, *Alcuin and Charlemagne: Studies in Carolingian History and Literature* (Ithaca, 1959); A. F. West, *Alcuin and the Rise of the Christian Schools* (New York, 1892).

[10] Clark, "Reappearance," pp. 17-24.

valuable manuscripts, but, alas, also for the accumulation and transmission of much of the textual corruption and erroneous or misleading information.[11]

Niccoli's chief agent was Poggio who was therefore a central figure in the humanistic movement in Italy. The tale of his search for classical manuscripts under the direction of Niccoli is quite astounding and immensely revealing. Poggio went to Constance in 1414 as one of the secretaries of Pope John XXIII. When his official work as secretary was over he conducted his searches. He sent numerous manuscripts, some of them unique, back to Niccoli, which he had often through questionable means discovered at the Abbey of Cluny, at St. Gall, at Langres, Cologne, Mainz and elsewhere.

Poggio hired scribes or induced monks to copy the manuscripts he found, since by this time it was rare that an abbot would allow a manuscript to be removed from his keeping. He complained continually about the *"ignorantissmus omnium viventium"* who copied his manuscripts, saying it would be necessary to have them re-copied by someone learned. He would himself make emmendations from the original: "So it will be easy for a good writer to detect similar errors and to correct them in other books." The range and extent of Poggio's efforts is reflected in the large library he developed for himself. It records the extraordinary story of the vigorous search for classical texts.[12]

THE MEDIEVAL *Artes Poeticae*

The interest in verse and the use of metrical form prompted the literary prescriptions of the 12th and 13th centuries. They were little more than exercise books providing practical assistance to the student and no doubt for the teacher, since like the *accessus* they were professorial guides. These school manuals produced versifiers of considerable technical skill who reworked old themes with elegant prolixity, their primary source being the classical authors thus revived and preserved.

The latter half of the twelfth and most of the thirteenth century contain the rise and focus of *artes poeticae*. Its most significant matter is contained in works of five writers. The major influence on all was the Roman grammatical tradition.[13] The dominant influence was Cicero considered the most read classical author in the Middle Ages. The authoritative *Rhetorica ad Herennium* was for a long time erroneously attributed to him. Other major influences were Donatus and Priscian.[14]

---

[11] *Ibid.*, pp. 24 ff.

[12] *Ibid.*, p. 36.

[13] The *De Nuptiis Philologiae et Mercurri* of Martianus Capella was one of the most important conveyers of Roman thought regarding liberal education.

[14] *Rhetorica ad Herennium*, ed. and trans. Harry Caplan, Loeb Classical Library, 1954; the *Ars Grammatica* and *Donati de Partibus Orationis: Ars Minor* are edited by H. Keil, *Grammatici Latini* 4 (Leipzig, 1864); Priscian's *Institutionum Grammaticarum* is also edited by H. Keil in *Grammatici Latini* 2 (Leipzig, 1855) and 3 (Leipzig, 1859).

In England Geoffrey of Vinsauf and John of Garland are the notable compilers of *artes poeticae*. Geoffrey's precepts are contained in the *Poetria Nova, Documentum de Modo et Arte Dictandi et Versificandi* and *Summa de Coloribus Rhetoricis.*[15] The *Documentum,* no doubt written after the *Poetria,* sets forth in prose essentially the same doctrine. As might be expected, the rewriting of the material reflects his second thought on some items, and in many instances the prose offers a clearer and more effective expression of his ideas. Therefore, it is perhaps the most satisfying representative text of the *artes peoticae.*[16] The *Summa,* a compilation of definitions and examples, is a separate discussion of the rhetorical colors. These works were probably composed shortly after 1200.

John of Garland produced *Parisiana Poetria de Arte Prosaica, Metrica, et Rithmica* and *Exampla Honestae Vitae.* He wrote numerous other works including several on grammar and rhetoric as well as a number of poems.[17] The *Parisiana Poetria* is another rhetorical treatise in the manner of Geoffrey's *Poetria* with an additional section on *ars dictaminis* and one on *ars rithmica.* His main sources are the *ad Herennium* and Horace. The *Exampla* is a collection of some sixty-four rhetorical devices with appropriate examples.

The *Laborintus* of Eberhard the German is a considerably shorter work than those mentioned and like them exhibits a preoccupation with rhetorical ornamentation through figures. A final section lists authors recommended for study and imitation. The list includes Alain of Lille's *Anticlaudianus,* Geoffrey's *Poetria Nova,* Vendôme's *Ars Versificatoria* and the works of Sidonius, Martianus Capella and Bernard Silvester.[18]

Gervais of Melkley's *Ars Versificaria* presents little that is new. His attempt for originality is reflected in an effort to achieve a fresh organization of matter stating that the bases of the various ornaments of style are derived from their expression of the "identity," and "similarity," or the "contrast" of things. The final part briefly surveys invention and arguments, adding comments on the rules concerning metrics and letter writing. He draws from Cicero, Donatus, Priscian, Cornificius, Bernard Silvester, Matthew and Geoffrey.[19]

---

[15] For texts see Edmond Faral, *Les Arts Poétiques du XIIe et du XIIIe Siècle,* Librairie Ancienne Honore Champion (Paris, 1924; reprinted Paris, 1971); see also *Poetria Nova,* trans. Margaret F. Nims (Toronto, 1967) and *Documentum de Modo et Arte Dictandi et Versificandi,* trans. Roger P. Parr (Milwaukee, 1968).

[16] The tendency of modern scholars to prefer the hexameter *Ars Poetica* rests perhaps on the fact that the text itself is an example of versification.

[17] For text see Traugott F. Lawler, ed. and trans. "John of Garland's *Parisiana Poetria de Arte Prosaica, Metrica, et Rithmica:* An Edition (Excluding the *Ars Rithmica*) with Translation, Introduction, and Notes," unpublished Ph. D. thesis, Harvard University, 1966.

[18] For text see Faral, *Arts Poétiques,* pp. 337-371; also Evelyn Carlson, trans. "The *Laborintus* of Eberhard rendered into English with Introduction and Notes," unpublished M.A. thesis, Cornell University, 1930.

[19] Text: Hans-Jurgen Grabner, ed. *Ars Poetica* in *Forschungen zur Romanischen Philologie* 17 (Munster, 1965); for a brief outline of the *Ars* see Faral, pp. 328-330.

Matthew of Vendôme and the Schools of Orleans

The earliest of these five writers of *artes poeticae* was Matthew of Vendôme. His *Ars Versiflcatoria* here translated was composed before 1175.[20] Very little biographical data is known about Matthew.[21] He says himself he was born in Vendôme. Faral states that he went to Tours where he was brought up by an uncle, and it was here that he was likely to have benefited from the tutelage of Bernard Silvester. After Tours he went to Orleans, possibly on the advice of Bernard, for Hugh Primus was flourishing there at that time.[22] Matthew taught grammar at Orleans, and as evidenced in his *Ars,* he seems to have been the object of what he calls "slanderous" attacks by Arnulf, possibly the reason he fled Orleans for Paris after finishing his treatise. Matthew's reply is equally slanderous as he accuses Arnulf of artistic jealousy, and his *Ars* is marred by his incautious retaliations, though they do liven an otherwise fairly dull treatise. He resided in Paris for about ten years where according to his own words he placed himself under the protection of the second Bishop Barthelmy and his brother.

Matthew's *Ars Versificatoria* is valuable certainly as an example of the standard *artes poeticae* and because it is the earliest of known texts. It holds a greater value, perhaps, for the insight it affords of the realistic human foibles it reveals, particularly among intellectuals. It was written as a reply to what he calls the envious emnity of a slanderer with whom he appears to have had a running feud.[23] The slanderer is continually referred to as Rufus or Rufinus identified at the conclusion as *Arnulfus de Sancto Evurcio.*[24] The opening and the conclusion of the treatise contain direct attacks, and throughout the work he seizes every opportunity to defame his rival, particularly when he offers illustrative examples of his own. Indeed, such examples, coming as they often do after a prolix list of illustrations from classic authors, reveals that the addition of his *domesticum exemplum* is precisely for the opportunity it affords to demolish Arnulf. It is made clear that all references to Rufus or Rufinus are barbs for his enemy. This relentless preoccupation does impair the work, however amusing it is for an audience. The feud was infamous enough to be referenced by Eberhard in the next century who seems to have agreed with Matthew.[25] As Bruno Roy points out the name Arnulf itself contained negative connotations which surely delighted Matthew.[26] How the spirited controversy must have amused the students and intellectuals of the day.

---

[20] Text: Faral, pp. 109-193.

[21] See Faral, pp. 1 ff.

[22] Berthe M. Marti, "Hugh Primas and Arnulf of Orléans," *Speculum* 30 (1955), pp. 233-238; L. Delisle, "Les Ecoles d'Orléans au xiie et au xiiie Siècle," *Annuaire-Bulletin de la Société de l'Histoire de France* 7 (1869), pp. 139-154.

[23] See *Ars,* Prologue.

[24] *Ars,* IV, 47.

[25] *Laborintus,* 675 ff.

[26] "Arnulf of Orleans and the Latin 'Comedy,' " *Speculum,* (Apr., 1974), p. 263., n. 39.

Arnulf of Orleans is known primarily for his glosses on classical authors including Lucan's *Pharasalia,* Ovid's *Metamorphoses, Ars Amatoria, Remedia Amoris, Ex Ponto* and others, the only works of his that appear to have survived, though it is likely that he wrote poetry and perhaps drama.[27] Roy thinks it was his poetry which caused the rivalry.[28] Faral establishes that it is unlikely that Matthew wrote the *Miles* [29] as had been thought, and Roy suggests the author was Arnulf.[30] The evidence is persuasive, though perhaps not final.

ACADEMIC CONTROVERSY: RHETORIC VERSUS POETRY

The feud between Matthew of Vendôme and Arnulf of Orleans has caught the attention and imagination of scholars. It is very likely that a fuller investigation of this feud might show it to have a significance beyond its surface amusement. Arnulf was the most popular and exciting teacher in Orleans. The immense task of investigating carefully his commentaries which were presumably lecture notes might reveal literary attitudes and ideas quite different from those considered standard for the age. The problem is that he "appears" to follow the general theory and mode of the schools. Indeed, investigators such as Marti, on one hand make this clear and at the same time attest considerable originality.[31] His commentaries, already indicative of his individuality, suggest that his oral presentation went considerably further. Arnulf incurred numerous enemies, most notably, of course, Vendôme and Hugh the Primate. They may have first envied his popularity with students and second resented his originality.

Artistic jealousy is a most common cause for pedagogical rivalry. The innovator is a gadfly; his persistent vision and his obsession with new truths is a constant threat to the pedant and the imitator. A review of Arnulf's commentaries suggest he was unusual and original for his time. He is said to be representative of his age and its spirit. This is undoubtedly true, but there are signs that he was also pointing the way to a new spirit concerning literature and literary theory. For instance, it would seem his method of teaching literary theory by minute analysis of the great works is sounder than that of the standard *artes poeticae* which recommends a dull systematized grammatical method through imitation of form. The tail seems definitely to be wagging the dog. One moves from effect; the other

---

[27] For texts and translations of Lucan and Ovid see Loeb Classical Library series; see also Berthe Marti, ed., *Arnulphi Aurelianensis Glosule super Lucanum* (Rome, 1958), pp. xv-xxix; M. Hadas, "Later Latin Epic and Lucan," *Cl. Weekly* 29 (1936); J. W. Basore, "Direct Speech in Lucan as an Element of Epic Technic," *Translations and Proceedings of the American Philological Association* 35 (1904), xciv; A. Gregorius, *De M. A. Lucani Pharsaliae Tropis* (Leipzig, 1893).

[28] *Op. cit.,* p. 263.

[29] "Le Fabliau Latin au Moyen Âge," *Romania,* L (1924), pp. 321-385.

[30] *Op. cit.* pp. 264-266.

[31] Glosule super Lucanum, pp. xxix-xxxvii.

towards effect. It is a truism that the great poet is an innovator in that he is directed by his own perception and vision rather than by a philosopher's or theorist's rule. It is also true that the degree of slavish imitation indicates the lessening degree of artistic power. Such is a would-be poet. The great artist is most consistently influenced by the vision of other artists more profoundly than he is by rule. Arnulf's commentaries reveal a tenacious attempt to present all possible interpretations, thus leading the students to discover meaning in terms of their own identity. His commentary on the *Pharsalia* is the starting point for developments on subjects of the *trivium*. Mari states that though Arnulf was at times pedantic, even long winded, his glosses are more often lucid, original, straightforward and concise.

Arnulf's philosophical views were greatly influenced by the Neoplatonic doctrine of William of Conches and his disciples. This suggest the possibility that he differed considerably from the accepted standard thinking of the time. Further, his range of knowledge was extensive, and he seems to have subscribed to numerous new theories: the conception of nature, the movement of the universe and its planets, the nature of the soul. Distinctive is his belief in the essential interrelation and evolution of being. Philosophy, astronomy, mathematics, astrology are interlocking disciplines for him. Little wonder that he notes that Lucan often spoke as a poet and not as a philosopher. The persistent detail with which he glosses might represent not mere pedantry but the fever with which he searched for truth which he attempted to convey to the student, indicating his view of the essential unity of being and the spirit which animates it.

It was thought that Arnulf's display of erudition was a matter of pride, impartially putting side by side the contradictory interpretations of his authorities. There is truth in this statement, no doubt. It might, however, reflect a view of poetry unlike the standard contemporary notion. Certainly the deeper poetic insight which animates a work prompted by poetic inspiration or perception would be illuminated by the manner in which the poet makes the parts work with each other. Arnulf's commentaries certainly bear further investigation for what they might reveal of his concept of poetry and consequently his literary theory.[32]

Arnulf refers to the concept of poetic inspiration in the *Accessus* to the commentary on the *Pharsalia*. Lucan, he says, is both historian and poet.[33] Surely Arnulf's statement that poets sing because they have been divinely inspired and thus write in metrics reveals a concept of poetry quite apart from that revealed by the standard *artes poeticae*. This, says Arnulf, quite justifies Lucan's use of the verb *cano* at the beginning of the poem. Clearly he distinguishes form and the animating spirit which gives it life, revealing his awareness of poet versus versifier. His statement that Lucan performed

---

[32] F. Ghisalberti thinks the rivalry between Arnulf and Matthew of Vendôme was caused by their different concepts of literature; cf. his "Arnolfo d'Orléans, un Cultore di Ovidio nel Secolo XII," in *Memorie del R. Istituto Lombardo di Scienze e Lettere* 24 (1932), pp. 157-234.

[33] *Glosule super Lucanum*, p. xxxviii; see also M.P.O. Morford, *The Poet Lucan* (Oxford, 1967); B. M. Marti, "The Meaning of the *Pharsalia*," *American Journal of Philology* 66 (1945).

his ethical function by making virtue attractive through the action of his heroes rather than by teaching morals shows more insight into the nature of poetry than is found in most literary commentaries of his time. It also indicates the reason for his popularity among students and the prejudice of his peers.

Arnulf records that historians and philosophers seek to establish truth and clearly state their views and conclusions. Lucan, he says, suggests many possible explanations of facts and occurrences, but does not attempt to choose among them or give a precise and final answer. It is this concept which motivates his setting forth of many possible interpretations.

Arnulf seems to have disagreed with the standard criticism of Lucan that his work illustrated rhetorical declamation rather than epic narrative. This critical attitude developed because Virgil was a major influence and he was unable to meet Virgil's poetic power in either subject or epic unity. It is true that Lucan was not a great poet, but he seems to have recognized the essential difference between orator and poet, and his work shows persistent attempts to achieve poetic power. It reveals, also, both his thorough rhetorical training and his desire for poetic expression. Thus his writing by including both of these elements is weakened by the lack of consistent narrative mode and epic unity. Such weaknesses appear to prompt the judgement of the majority of his critics.[34]

Arnulf's view of this standard critical reaction to Lucan is analogous to his own attitude concerning the *artes poeticae*. He seems to have been conscious of the true nature of Lucan's work prompting his determination to teach the difference between rhetoric and poetry.

The poetic achievement of Lucan is reflected in the nature and quality of his dramatic narrative and his desire for distinctive characterization by emphasizing the reality of man's difficulty in adjusting to life's evolving problems. Thus many of his characterizations reflect the desire to replace traditional descriptive method and language with that which reflected contemporary views.

Lucan's original intention seems clear though his rhetorical training rendered it difficult to maintain throughout his work. His writing also reflects the maturity of his views on standard subjects and his attempt to humanize by dramatic narrative. Though his greatest influence was Virgil, he wished to avoid imitation and used Virgil instead as a source of originality in an effort to reflect contemporary views. Arnulf's interest in Ovid and Lucan suggests the same desire to avoid tradition and bring to poetry its natural facility for extensive variety of implied meaning. This is reflected in his commentaries on the works of both writers.

The period following Virgil clearly reflects the literary controversy between rhetoric and poetry. Arnulf's persistent interest in Ovid and Lucan reflects his awareness of this controversy. It seems very likely, therefore,

---

[34] E. M. Sanford, "Lucan and His Roman Critics," *Classical Philology* 26 (1931); M. Hadas, "Later Latin Epic and Lucan," *Cl. Weekly* 29 (1936).

that his teaching popularity may have been in part the result of his effort to free poetry from the traditional rhetorical prison reflected in the imitation theory which characterizes the *artes poeticae.* He was no doubt aware of the fact that the schools of declamation were the only available training places for poets. The major source of such schools was Virgil. Ovid and Lucan were both victims of such rhetorical influence. Arnulf felt that a similar influence was limiting and misleading the students of his time as a result of the *artes poeticae* whose primary aim was the revival and purification of the Latin Language.

One sees in Arnulf's commentaries and in the antagonism which flourished in Orleans an attempt of one individual to break, not from the established rules of writing, but from the rigid and limited concept of the logical basis of literature which formed *ars grammaticus.* Like Chaucer, Arnulf perhaps represents a new spirit, a fuller view. Both point to a new age while yet vividly reflecting the cumulative achievements of the past. Others there were who also stood on the ridge of two dynamic ages and with two distinct views discernible in their art. The evolution of new thought is consistently projected in evolving medieval form. Thus we realize the transitional nature of the times and their work. Artistic development did not move forward as a direct break with contemporary poetic. The great artist reflects both the age and the landscape he transcends. As he points to new horizons he is sensitive to the still unfelt tremors of developing thought. He is influenced by his age precisely because he is an artist. He also becomes the source of influence to succeeding ages by virtue of his advanced and keen insight and the strength and persistence of his artistic focus and energy.

Matthew of Vendôme, like Hugh, the Primate, considered Arnulf a pedant and his verses uncouth, while thinking of himself as a poet endowed with imagination and creative power. His own poetry and treatise reveal it is unlikely that he can be believed. His attacks on Arnulf, no doubt amusing to his students, are grotesque examples to illustrate grammatical rules and rhetorical devices, without imagination and revealing no suggestion of poetic power. Indeed, throughout the treatise his own examples are singularly banal, compared to those taken from the "authors."

One wonders too if Vendôme's hatred of Arnulf might have stemmed in part from the general abhorrence of pagan literature which existed at the time. We know from Deslisle and Haureau[35] that Arnulf was defamed by Alexander of Villedieu in the prologue of his *Ecclesiale,* written at the turn of the century – 1199-1202. Alexander excoriated the pernicious pagan doctrine taught through the Roman poets in the schools of Orleans, particularly Ovid. Arnulf not only wrote commentaries on most of Ovid's works, but is thought to have written a life of Ovid. Small wonder his peers objected to the infusion of Ovid's ideas, particularly to youthful students. Alexander considered his *Ecclesiale* a Christian *Fasti* designed to counteract

---

[35] B. Haureau, *Histoire Littéraire de la France* 29 (1885), pp. 573-81.

the sway of Ovid's works and the influence of its disciples at Orleans. He charged a certain unnamed Magister of Orleans of leading astray his students by exposure of the pagan authors. As Marti suggests, it is very likely he is referring to Arnulf, the noted commmentator on the *Fasti*.

It is possible that Arnulf's criticism of Vendôme's verse reflects an awarenes of the difference between poet and versifier. Careful scrutiny of the *Tobias* supports this criticism. Obviously he considered Matthew a versifier. The awareness of this distinction can be seen perhaps in the commentary on Lucan where he compares the Etruscans in the art of intuitive perception after they had been taught by Tages, to the fame gained by Orleans through the reputation of Hilary.[36] Interest in Ovid might also reflect a preference for poetic perception over mere verse. Isadore of Seville names Ovid as the Pagan author most to be avoided.[37] While Ovid is certainly a skillful rhetorician, he also knew how to tingle the emotions and release the imagination and feelings which were rather rigidly restrained by a zealous Church. Ovid's mode was magic, bestowing as it did a certain nobility to careless ease and sensuous delight.

Arnulf was also throughly disliked by a certain Fulco, a *scholasticus,* probably at the cathedral school of Orleans.[38] Circumstances surrounding this antagonism also need further investigation to identify whether or not it was prompted by Arnulf's emphasis of Pagan works. Hugh Primas of Orleans also attacks Arnulf in his own collection of verses. The reason given that he had been swindled by Arnulf in a dice game seems a flimsy cover indeed. The point is that we are not at present in a position to know for certain whether the attacks against Arnulf were justified and what their true basis was. The likelihood is fairly strong that they were the result of artistic jealousy stemming from his popularity, his challenging individuality, perhaps even because he disagreed on current standard *artes poeticae* and was introducing new and dangerous elements into literature which should not be taught to the young. Gisalberti is perhaps correct in thinking the rivalry stemmed primarily from divergent views of literature. He thought Arnulf viewed the classic texts with the freshness and independence of a poet.

In the various conflicting reports of Arnulf's literary virtues, one fact remains clear. His personality is marked throughout. His direct and rather conversational style remains his own. One is reminded of this singular trait as pertaining also to Chaucer and the *Pearl* Poet. It reveals the exception not the rule. Surely such exceptions also reflect the influence of the *artes poeticae*. Their greatness in a measure can be gauged by the degree of success with which they subjected the accumulated ideas and techniques of the past and of their age to their own independent vision. By this standard most medieval writers fail to impress. They remain in the background of their

---

[36] I. 584; Hilary was responsible for introducing classical studies at Orleans.

[37] W. M. Lindsay, ed. *Etymologiarum sive Originum Libri* XX, 2 vols. (Oxford, 1911); Dorothy V. Cerino, "The Rhetoric and Dialectic of Isidorus of Seville: A Translation and Commentary," unpublished M.A. thesis, Brooklyn College, 1938.

[38] Marti, *Glosule super Lucanum,* pp. xxvi-xxvii.

work which consists in the laborious construction of rhetorical mosaic. The texts of the *artes poeticae* also reveal that it is a mistake to consider them as literary works of merit. Sedgwick's careful analysis prompted his view that they are for the most part dull school manuals attempting to achieve the elegance of verse. A detailed analysis of Matthew of Vendôme's *Ars Versificatoria* reveals that Bolgar is giving faint praise when he says that the *Ars* "is at once a typical example of the genre and more competently written than the rest." [39] Indeed, a contrary view was expressed by Haureau who called Matthew, "le plus prolixe, le plus banal des poètes du XIIᵉ siècle, le plus laborieux artisan de frivoles antithèses." [40]

---

[39] *The Classical Heritage* (New York, 1954), p. 211.

[40] *Journal des Savants* (1883), p. 212.

THE ART

OF

THE VERSEMAKER

[PROLOGUE]

1.   Were envy to cease, the enemy of the one from Vendome
        Would not criticize an introductory work.

Not to seem to over-play my tassels,[1] I have long delayed a work I proposed to do. But because delay is the stepmother[2] of covenant, may I not
seem as a dissembler of my own power and as serving only myself,[3] after
righting the plumbline of reason, and in keeping with the insignificance of
my feeble talent, I have wished to convert my promise into accomplishment
so as to promote theory, increase learning, furnish food for envy, agony for
enmity, and nourishment for slander. **2.** Indeed, I grant to my detractors
time for deliberation so that only after consulting where discernment abides
and first learning the occasion and the thinking leading to my writing, they
may apply their undiscerning preconceptions to this little work with an
overbold bite. Long silence nourishes expression and impetuosity always
serves poorly.[4] Hence, let my mutual adversary Rufinus,[5] the disgrace of
men and the outcast of the masses,[6] set a watch on his mouth and a door to
attend on his lips;[7] and let him not by kindling his envy present us with
impulsive abuse of my writing without any of reason's discernment; but let
him sport in his concubine's quarters and embrace red-haired Thais.

3.   If Rufinus gnaws at my verses, a ruddiness
        Can be the herald of his wicknedness.
     His voice re-echoes his skin, his tongue mocks his color.
        In Rufus ruddy-colored faithfulness is restless.[8]

For my part I am not envious:

     If he has held me up in my scholarship, albeit for a price,
        Let a ruddy she-goat hold up Rufus the male.

---

[1] Cf. Matt. xxiii. 5; Deut. vi. 8. These "frontlets" or "phylacteries" which contained important words of scripture were rolled up in a case of black calfskin which was attached to a stiff
leather thong about one inch wide and twenty inches long. They were attached to the bend of
the left arm. Shorter thongs were worn on the forehead. The expression "they make broad
their phylacteries" refers to the Pharisees who wore them as conspiciously as possible. Cf. also
Deut. xi. 18 and Numbers, xv.38.

[2] *Noverca* or stepmother: eventually malevolent or hostile.

[3] Cf. Horace, *Ep.*I. 9. 9.

[4] Cf. Statius, *Theb.* X. 704.

[5] Rufinus indicated a red-haired man or one with a ruddy complexion and came to be the
sign of wickedness or deceit. Matthew himself indentifies Rufus as Arnulf of St. Evurcius who
had irritated him "with daily insult." See IV, 47.

[6] Cf. *Ps.* xxi. 7.

[7] Cf. *Ps.* xxxviii. 2.

[8] See I. 22 and II. 42 for explanation of line.

Since he cannot bite, he should be more sparing in his barbs. **4.** Moreover, let not the novelty of the little work be ascribed to over-boldness, for neither the desire for favor nor the ostentation of vainglory effects it, but instruction for the less advanced does, so that the credit the execution of the work cannot wrench forth, the affection of the worker may. **5.** Therefore, since I am bound by contract, and postponement always hurts those who are ready,[9] I purpose not to seem to be replying to the ever-expectant bumpkin. About this Horace:

> The bumpkin waits for the river to flow out, but
> It flows and will flow and roll on forever,[10]

since the ripe hour has come for my narratives, to have Rufus' sides burst with envy, I approach the introductory work with such commitment that if in the following treatise no small spark of charm has not crept in, and if someone while returning evil for good and offering a gift of unmerited recompense has presumed to snigger, may his sterile and unfruitful prating be punished by an arrow flying through the day, uneasy tossing through the night, etc.[11] **6.** Although I have chosen for myself a personal and familiar path in the practice of versification, because I am ashamed to go a handed-down way and it is wretched to lean upon another's reputation, still I do not presume in this segment to erode the knowledge of others by censorious abrasion. What's more, if anyone, suffering from the fault of neglectfulness, will consider the following of little value, or what is easy, if a prejudgment of my ability as versemaker will be found, I do not wait for the slow nor harass those going ahead.[12] **7.** Further, stitchers of patches should be excluded from examining this work. When many are the versifiers called but few the chosen,[13] some rely on the title alone and pant according to the meter of the verses rather than the beauty of what is in meter. Some merely rearrange the patchwork line which throws the shadow of a trunk, not of foliage, and strive to pound into a unit an aggregate of triffles, which because of their own deformity do not dare to go out in public, and seem to take turns among themselves in shouting:

> We are numbers only, born to consume the fruits
> of the earth.[14]

---

[9] Cf. Lucan, *The Civil War,* I, 281; this poem was originally called *The Pharsalia,* which is not accurate since it applies only to the events in Book VII. The manuscript title is *De Bello Civili.* It is thought the words *Pharsalia nostra,* ix. 985, inaccurately interpreted as "my poem, the Pharsalia," prompted the mistake.

[10] *Ep.* I. 2. 42.

[11] Cf. Ps. 91. 6-7; ". . . and from attack by the noonday devil." The quotation was part of daily compline which everyone in the Middle Ages knew by heart. Matthew habitually gives only a part of very familiar sayings.

[12] Cf. Hor. *Ep.* I. 2. 71.

[13] Math. XXII. 14.

[14] Hor. *Ep.* I. 2. 27.

[I. CONCERNING IDEAS]

1. Since the present concern looks to introducing verses, a verse ought to be described in some way. A verse is metrical language moving along succinctly and clause by clause in a graceful marriage of words and depicting thoughts with the flowers of rhetoric, containing in itself nothing played down, nothing idle. A collection of utterances, measured feet, the knowledge of quantities do not constitute a verse, but the elegant joining of utterances does, the expression of distinctive features and respect for the designation of each and every thing.

2. The designation given something substantive is accidental; it pertains to good or evil, or something indifferent: to evil as

> An aged Laertes,[1]

because, as Horace testifies,

> Many troubles encompass an aged man;[2]

to good, as

> The boy Telemachus,[3]

because boy rejoices in his nimbleness: to the indifferent, as

> The white swan sings to the waters of the Maeanderer[4]

since to be white or black indicates neither a good nor an evil.

3. In the practice of the discipline of versification, a beginning of the matter is made in two ways, and a rather elegant beginning is possible. There are, however, four other ways which we, as it were, reject and leave for those of ailing eyes and barbers.[5] But we have set forth the first two for the listener's choice.

---

[1] Ovid, *Her.* I. 98.

[2] *Ars Poetica*, 169.

[3] Ovid, *Her.* I. 98.

[4] Ovid, *Ep.* VII. 2.

[5] Cf. Horace, *Sat.* I. 7. 3; cf. also Part II. 23.

4. One way is to begin with the use of zeugma. Zeugma occurs when diverse clauses are united by the expression of a single verb.

5. Indeed, zeugma has three variations. Zeugma is created at the beginning, at the middle and at the end.[6]

6. At the beginning, when a verb placed in the first clause is understood to be repeated in each of the succeeding clauses; as in Ovid:

> Cold was struggling with hot, moist with dry,
> Soft with hard, weightless with weighty.[7]

7. To cite my own example, if there be question of applauding the female sex, one should begin as follows:

> Parasis is celebrated for her fondness for the bow.
>   Luxuriating with a reflection of Spring's figure, rich in ancestry.

8. If there is question of criticism of the female sex, one should begin thus:

> Of the female sex Medea is the scum, the ruin of justice
> The disgrace of the world, a sick plague.

9. Similar will be the beginning of applause or criticism of the masculine sex: For applause, thus:

> Caesar is celebrated for his renown in war, support
>   Of the honorable, prudence in counsel, power in the city.

10. In criticism, thus:

> Verres is defiled with the vice of theft, the absence
>   Of virtue, the tendency to plunder, indolence in war.

11. Zeugma at the end occurs when a verb placed in the last clause refers to the preceding clauses; thus:

> You a master, you a husband, you a brother were to me.

Not to seem too generous with examples, after citing a single authentic author,[8] let one of my own making suffice. This is clearly for praise:

> For extraordinary character, for beauty of face,
>   For kindly address, for title of descent, Ino is celebrated.

---

[6] Also called *conjunction* (*Zeugma a medio*): connecting two clauses by placing a single verb between them: *adjunctio* indicating before or after connecting: *zeugma a superiori* when clauses are linked by placing a verb at the beginning of the first clause, and *zeugma ab inferiori* when the verb is placed at the end of the second clause.

[7] *Met.* I. 19-20.

[8] The rebirth of Latin studies is reflected in the numerous references to authentic or standard classical authors. Thus Matthew of Vendome like Geoffrey of Vinsauf and others provided handbooks to aid the schoolmaster with his task of teaching Latin verse. Classical authors provided unlimited examples for imitation, and contributes to the monotonous similarity of subject matter and treatment.

Similar will be the beginning critical of the masculine sex, with a change of words but the mode of speaking kept.

12. Zeugma from the middle occurs when a verb placed in the middle between preceding and following clauses refers to both sides, as in Statius:

> Shield by shield, boss by boss is repelled,
> Threatening sword by sword, foot by foot and spear by spear.[9]

Similarly concerning the Earthborn who killed one another:

> They are perishing for whom beginning is end, for whom
> To be is not to be, for whom the first day is last.

13. In the second way the matter begins with hypozeuxis.[10] Hypozeuxis is a figure contrary to zeugma since it assigns a verb to each single clause, as in the passage in Statius:

> She lusts for war, and she loosens her jaws
> and sets her talons.[11]

To give my own example, in praising a leader or a king one should begin thus:

> Preeminence of character gives title to Agenor,
> Virtue eulogizes him, ability distinguishes him,
> fame blesses him.

Likewise about the matter of the female sex:

> Charm of character beautifies Penelope, a queenly bearing
> Reveals her, the fullness of her virtues enrich her.

14. Hypozeuxis is said to be, as it were, the contrary figure of zeugma, because in the zeugmatic beginning, several clauses are constructed with a single verb as is evident in the examples already seen; with hypozeuxis, on the other hand, each and every single clause is assigned its own verb.

15. Also metonomy frequently ought to be used in beginning the matter, as when a characteristic of the thing contained would be attributed to the space containing it (or the opposite), as follows:

> Thebes celebrates the festivals of Bacchus, the pius crowd
> Visits in numbers the rites of the god, honors again the
> temples, and burns incense.

The thing contained for the container, as in Lucan:

---

[9] *Thebaid,* VIII. 398-99.

[10] Known also as *disjunctio* or *disjunctum.*

[11] *Theb.* II. 130.

> The Sequani,[12] an excellent nation, who excel in wheeling their
> bridled steeds.[13]

for here the stream stands for the region in which it is located. The former
mode is included under hypozeuxis when each and every clause is assigned
its own verb.

16. Procedure with a General Statement or Proverb. For
one to employ zeugmatic beginning or even according to hypozeuxis, one
ought to set down first a general proverb, that is, a general idea, to which
credence is customarily given, common opinion renders assent, and by
which the integrity of uncorrupted truth is undisturbed. **17.** Indeed, if one
must treat the instability of fortune, it can be placed before such a proverb:

> The deceptive favor of Fortune nods according to circumstances,
>   Fate knows not how to perpetuate trust in stability.
> The wheel of fortune is uncertain, unstable; indeed,
>   Faith in fate is not to have had faith.
> Everything of man's hangs by a slender thread,
>   And by sudden misfortune the strong collapse.[14]

18. If one must treat of the misfortune in love, one can thus apply the
proverb:

> Reason departs into exile, the plumb line of justice
>   Goes awry; there wild love domineers.
> Love distinguishes no priority, liberty is a slave to love,
>   Love knows not how to spare even the gods.

Therefore Ovid says:

> It reigns and holds its law to have dominion over the gods.[15]

19. In treating the halfheartedness of a promise which torments the expec-
tant, thus:

> The directly given gift is more pleasing, A giver's
>   Slow hand is usually merit's mother-in-law.

Hence Lucan:

> Let whatever you intend be sudden.[16]

Hence the apostle: "God loves a joyous giver."[17]

---

[12] In ancient history a people of eastern Gaul who dwelt east of the Celtic Aedui and west of
the Jura.

[13] *Phars.* I. 425.

[14] Ovid. *Pont.* IV. 3.

[15] *Her.* IV. 12.

[16] *Phars.* II. 14.

[17] Cf. *Cor.* II. 9. 7.

20. In treating imperfect happiness which is an affliction of human life, thus:

> Imperfection has a companion that is envious of human affairs:
>   All prosperity lacks integrity.

Horace:

> Nothing is happy in every respect.[18]

Cato:

> No one lives without reproach.

21. About ingenuity which usually grows with affliction, thus:

> Sorrow increases the resources of talent and
>   Shrewd anxiety discerns more fully because of adversity.

Hence Ovid:

>   Sorrow has great talent and
> Shrewdness comes at times of wretchedness.[19]

22. On inconstancy of mind:

> Inconstancy of mind invites a loss of faith:
>   Trust seldom beats in a fickel breast.

23. Concerning the performance of wisdom which judges the outcome of things:

> It sets the goals and determines what and whence.

Hence Lucan:

>   Such was the character, such the unchanging life of
> Severe Cato, to maintain control and hold to the goal.[20]

24. Concerning the efficacy of fear:

> Fear assumes evil everywhere, augurs things to be feared,
>   And announces worse things than crises.

Hence Statius:

> Fear, the worst augur in perplexity, turns wheels everywhere.[21]

25. Concerning the rash repression of nature, thus:

> Indiscreet rashness does harm, is deceived, and errs,
>   Thinking to destroy a natural good.

---

[18] *Odes*, II. 16. 28.
[19] *Met.* VI. 574
[20] *Phars.* II. 380-81.
[21] Cf. *Theb.* III. 6.

Hence Horace:

> Though one drive out nature with a pitchfork, she will
>   always return.[22]

26. Concerning the effect of habit:

> The manner of living reflects nature, the urn refuses
>   To forget the flavor which it got when new.

Hence Horace:

> The urn will long preserve the fragrance with which it
>   was once seasoned when new.[23]
> What the new urn captures, the old one smells of.

27. Or, because there is no personal nobility without virtue, thus:

> Virtue enobles the spirit; when virtue is removed
>   Love of nobility departs into exile.

Hence Claudian:

> It is becoming to rely on virtue, not blood.[24]
> Nobility of spirit is the sole and unique virtue.

28. Since the sin is more visible because of the standing of the sinner, thus:

> The renown of the sinner doubles the fault.
>   The honor of a fool's reputation deflates his fault.

Juvenal:

> Every defect of the soul has more conspicuous infamy in itself
> In proportion to the esteem enjoyed by the sinner.[25]

29. Concerning slavish wickedness, as follows:

> Slavish madness abounds in obsequiousness, ends in
>   Things forbidden, ignorant of justice, powerful in deceit.

In Claudian:

> There is nothing more grating than the lowly one on
>   surging to high estate.
> He strikes everything, for all the time he fears everything:
>   he vents his rage on all,
> So they will think he is powerful. Nor is any
> Beast more disgusting than a mad slave raging fury
>   at the backs of freemen:

---

[22] *Ep.* I. 10. 24.
[23] *Ep.* I. 2. 69.
[24] VIII. 220.
[25] *Sat.* VIII. 140-41.

Their groans are familiar to him, and he knows not to be
     sparing of punishment which
He himself has endured. Remembering his own master
     he hates him whom he strikes.[26]

Many other examples of this kind can be given.

30. Further, if one employs the zeugmatic beginning or the hypozeuxis beginning, three faults accompanying the beginning and the developing of the material are especially to be avoided, on the authority of Horace, namely: styles which are uneven and loose, verbose and inflated, dry and colorless.[27] **31.** Anyone while pursuing mediocrity in words, is either riding toward too great flourish in words, or is getting diverted to everyday words and those too plain, and thus falls into the fault of unevenness and looseness, that is, the fault of incoherence, as for example:

What is first differs from the middle, the middle also
     from the last.[28]

Horace condemns this defect, saying:

Force and spirit are lost to him pursuing smoothness.[29]

—32. The second fault occurs when one employs a superfluous flourish of words and ornamented speech and grasps at clouds and vacuities, because it would seem that no conclusion could respond in proportion to the splendor of the beginning. This fault is condemned by Horace when he says:

After announcing sublimity, he is bombastic.[30]

Elsewhere he sets forth an example of a "cyclic writer,"[31] using the bombastic and inflated beginning, saying:

I shall sing of the fate of Priam and the glorious war.[32]

Immediately he berates him for an exaggertated beginning, saying:

What will this boaster worthy of such mouth-gaping produce?
The mountains will be in labor, a ridiculous mouse will be born.[33]

---

[26] XVIII. 181-86.

[27] Faral notes that the precept is from *Ad Herennium;* for a discussion of style in Horace see *Ars Poetica* 24-37.

[28] Cf. *Ars. Poet.* 151-52. As the following references suggest there seems little doubt Matthew had a copy of Horace before him.

[29] *Ars Poet.* 26.

[30] *Ars Poet.* 27.

[31] *Ars Poet.* 136; one of the epic poets between 800 and 500 B.C. who treated in regular order the cycle of myths from the beginning to the time of Telemachus.

[32] *Ars Poet.* 137.

[33] *Ars Poet.* 138-39.

—**33.** The third fault, dry and bloodless, occurs when being too ordinary in our words, we overlook the slight ornaments of speech and elegance of meaning.[34] Horace, however, condemns this fault in quoting a metaphor taken from sailing:

> He creeps along the ground, too cautious and afraid of a
> storm.[35]

34. An imitation of ornateness and a certain restraint in words ought to be observed,

> lest you be the imitator who plunges into the deep,
> From where shame or the rules of your work forbid retreating.[36]

But by observing the characteristics of persons, let the development of the material

> be maintained to the last just as it set
> Out from the beginning and remained self-consistent,[37]

so that nothing be found of smaller dimensions, nothing idle.

35. There are other faults which Horace in the beginning of the *Ars Poetica* tells us to avoid; these, in order to evade lengthiness, a step-mother to memory, I pass over for the present and direct the attention of the listener to an investigation of the meaning of poetic discipline.

36. Further, in working out the material, the manifold similarity[38] of tenses is to be observed to avoid the occurance of a diverse change of style; but dissimilarity of tense, namely the incoherence of sentences, should be especially avoided except when there may have been an urgent reason, that is:

> Unless a difficulty may have happened worthy of solution.[39]

For when the instance of necessity presses, the rule suffers great injury. If a question about past and future is to be treated as if they were present and connected with current action, this too is to be treated with a certain accommodation of expression. He who uses verbs of the present tense proceeds succinctly and briefly. Uncomplicated brevity gets a friendly hearing.

---

[34] Referring to *figurae verborum* (word figures or figures of diction) and *figurae sententiarum* (figures of thought), a standard distinction among theorists though this distinction is not rigidly observed. Cf. Geoffrey of Vinsauf's *Poetria Nova,* 1099-1234 and 1235-1592.

[35] *Ars Poet.* 28.

[36] *Ars Poet.* 134-35.

[37] *Ars Poet.* 126-27.

[38] Sedgwick amends *dissimilitudo* to *similitudo:* "Notes and Emendations on Faral's Les Arts Poétiques du XII^c et XIII^c Siècle." *Speculum* 2, (1927) 349-81.

[39] *Ars Poet.* 191.

37. Moreover, an incongruous arrangement of parts is especially to be avoided, lest implicit expressions belonging to diverse utterances be also entangled. For such a confusion of words is a step-mother to understanding and offers an obstacle to teaching. Indeed, just as utterances in connected construction are close to one another, the versifier in meter, if possible, should use such order that the fault called cacosynthesis does not happen, that is poor positioning of words. *Kakos* means "bad," *synthesis* is from *sin* which means "with" or "like," and *thesis,* which means position.

38. Further, we must not omit the question whether the character being treated should be described or his description omitted. Frequently the description of a character is appropriate, very often, superfluous. **39.** For example, if the manliness of some character be the subject, his constancy of mind, his desire for honorability, his flight from servility, as the severity of Cato is treated in Lucan,[40] the myriad perfections of Cato should be described, so that the refinement of his character and the multifaceted personal nature of his virtue be heard, and whatever follows about the carelessness of Caesar, his regard for liberty, can more easily be told the auditor. **40.** Also, if the efficacy of love be discussed, as how Jupiter burned with love for Parasis, a description of the girl should be examined, and she should be credited with the elegance of girlish beauty so that, on hearing the picture of beauty, it is probable and conjectural to the hearer, as it were, that Jove's heart should sweat at charms so many and so great. For the abundance of beauty must have been overwhelming which drove Jove to the vice of ravishment.

41. Further, in description one ought to observe both the characteristics of persons and the diversity of characteristics. For one ought to note the characteristics of rank, age, occupation, of natural sex, natural location and the other characteristics called by Tullius the attributes of a person. **42.** Horace acknowledges this diversity of characteristics when he says:

> It will differ greatly whether it is Davus[41] who speaks, or
> a hero,

(An example of the diversity of rank);

> Whether a mature old man speaks or a stripling warm with
> Blooming youth,

(An example of the difference of age);

> whether an influential matron or an officious nurse,

(another example of the difference of rank in women);

> Whether a wandering merchant or a tiller of a verdant field,

---

[40] *Phars.* II. 380 ff. Cato's work on morals and other subjects has been lost, though he is much quoted by Cicero, Quintilian and Pliny.

[41] A conventional name for a slave in Latin comedies. Cf. Horace, *Satire* II. 5. 91: *Davus sis comicus atque, stes capite obstipo:* Act the Davus of the comedy and stand with head bowed.

(an example of the difference of occupation);

> A Colchian or an Asyrian,

(an example of the difference of race);

> One reared in Thebes or in Argos,[42]

(an example of the difference of city). **43.** Horace explains why such a delineation of characteristics should be made, saying:

> Lest by chance senile characteristics be assigned
> To youth and manly ones to a boy, we must always dwell
> On characteristics joined to and fitted to the time of life.[43]

44. However, everyone should be designated by that epithet which is strongest in him and for which he is best known, as in this example from Horace:

> If as writer you by chance again bring back the famed Achilles,
> Let him be indefatigable, full of wrath, inexorable, fierce.
> Let him deny that laws were made for him, and claim all
>   through force of arms.[44]

45. Also, the character of words should conform to the facial expression and inner status of the persons speaking. For

> Somber words become a dejected face,
> Threatening words an angry one, wanton words a
> Sportive one, and serious words a stern face.[45]

Horace amplifies with the reason why such suitability of words is to be observed:

> If words are ill-suited to the status of the speaker,
> The Roman horsemen and the pedestrians will raise guffaws aloft.[46]

But this seems to look especially to the manner of recitation.

46. Therefore, a description of a church shepherd is to be made in one way, of a general in another; of a girl in another, of an elderly woman, a matron, a concubine or a waiting-woman in other ways; that of a boy or young man in one way, of an elderly man in another; of a freedman in another, one in a limited state in another. Variations in other characteristics should be observed in descriptions: Horace calls these tones of the works.[47] **47.** Indeed, for greater clarity in the teaching, since a comparative example clarifies understanding, let the description of certain persons

---

[42] *Ars Poet.* 114 ff.

[43] *Ars Poet.* 176-78.

[44] *Ars Poet.* 120-22.

[45] *Ars Poet.* 105-07.

[46] *Ars Poet.* 112-13.

[47] *Ars Poet.* 86.

be set down as a basis with this agreement, that if many faults occur in the verses which follow, no criticism of my detractor revile me. **48.** For

> Sometimes good Homer nods,[48]
> Nor will the bow always hit what it threatens.[49]

But against the detractor Horace offers me consolation when he says:

> Indeed when a number of points gleam in a poem
> Not I shall be offended by a few blemishes
> Which either carelessness lets flow in or which
> Human nature guarded against too little.[50]

For an incidental fault is venial, but frequent fault is mortal; wherefore Horace says:

> It is not shameful to have indulged, but not to cut
> indulgence short.[51]

49. For this reason let it be understood that nothing in the following descriptions is said apodictically, but by way of examples.

50.   The world proceeds after the example of the Pope,
>   His virtue sparkles, his reason is combative, his rank
>   honored.
> Holy in religion, restrained in speech, he is a cultivator
>   Of the honorable, provident in counsel, the summit of the
>   world.
> He is concerned to furnish allowances, nor does his world
>   change
>   An adjective to its opposite meaning when the meaning is in
>   keeping with the sound.
> When he leads reason advances, wrath sits cooling,
>   Dutiful piety flowers into peace.
> His conversation resembles nothing human,
>   Rejecting the guilt of men and fixing the gaze on God.
> He condoles with the afflicted, is merciful to the wretched;
>   He eagerly pursues justice, represses crimes, cherishes
>   righteousness.
> The Pope teaches what should be taught, forbids what should
>   be forbidden,
>   Punishes the guilty, and bears the spiritual scepter.
> In this world he binds and loosens souls; by binding and
>   loosening
>   He performs the office of the heavenly shepherd.

---

[48] *Ars Poet.* 359.

[49] *Ars Poet.* 350.

[50] *Ars Poet.* 351-53.

[51] *Ep.* I. 14. 36.

He watches over us, his children, his flock, us his members,
  The head guarding its members, the father his charges,
      the pastor his sheep.
The assemblage of virtues contend within the Pope:
  Virtue struggles to sieze virtue's place first.
The virtues hold trial before the father:
  Each demands to be first fruits of the holy man.
Justice strives to precede moderation;
  Gentle piety struggles to appropriate the father for
      herself.
The fourth, wisdom, strives to lead the three, it contends
  Before the father, as quality does with quality, sister with
      sister;
Right stands firm, fidelity calms, equanimity keeps the peace.
  Observation conducts each and every activity on the straight.
The perfection of the Pope has these four virtues on as many
      sides:
  The quadrature is a toast to his status and renders fidelity
      unfailing.
Relying on these four sides he does not depart into crimes's use:
  And he knows not how to be unmindful of God.
The Pope rules rulers, as lord he is master, and orders
  Harsh princes to command according to established law.
He outstrips human value, and banishing fragile feelings
  He can light the way of man.
Since he extends his stride across humankind from the lost earth
  He looks ahead in his thoughts upon the journey to the
      heavenly fatherland.
He seeks to exchange the unstable for the stable,
  Delusions for certainty, the earth for heaven, and inn for a
      home.
His holy mind loathes its ailing vessel, his spiritual
  Mobility complains bitterly of being shackled to the flesh.
The conjoined flesh does not lessen the gifts of the mind.
  The bridegroom spirit seeks to aid his spouse, the flesh.
His mind thirsts for the heavenly abode, and as shepherd
  He visits with his body the inn of the earth, with his
      mind, heaven.
Accusations with a sacrilegious bite do not defame holy hearts.
  Nor may they depreciate worth.
He is good: he is better, he is best and it is sufficient
  That his goodness has been deserved in the quadrature.

51. The constancy of Caesar flashes in battle, he resists
      Opposition, shatters the strong, tames the savage.
  His compassion warms towards the afflicted, he reveals
      himself an
    Enemy to his enemies, and seeks to be gentle to the gentle.

He outshines leaders in valor, is an examplar of
  Knightly service; he excels in worth and leads in nobility.
He is first in straining for forbidden expeditions, sighs for a
  Soldier's work; he scoffs at rest and flies to combat.
He thirsts for wars and his sword he makes confederate
      to his side.
  His valor knows not of failure, his back ignorant of flight.
He delights to put his hope in his sword; justice is reaped with
  The sword as judge; with sword as protector he takes
      to the road.
Fortune bows to Caesar's nod; he holds an ambiguous
  Circumstance as the smile of fortune.
Caesar rises amid adversities, nor does the winter of
  Upset prosperity overwhelm his nobility of countenance.
He puts down the savage, cherishes the peaceful,
  And weighs together the vicissitudes of peace and villany with
      the balance of justice.
He combines law with gentle restraint, while he warms the
  Sword of judgement with the charms of affection.
Therefore restraint battles to keep gentleness
  From flattening the law, or the law disavow work of
      dedication.
The weight of his sovereignty does not impoverish his mind,
  But rather each particular virtue flies to its duty.
His endowment flowers with its gifts, he does not exile the arts,
  Nor do his concerns flee from imperial rule.
Neither his preeminence with the sceptor, the nobility
      of his mind,
  Nor the glory of his family, nor the mountain of his labors
Darken the brightness of his nature.
  His thirst for ambition does not impair his fidelity.
But rather his loving faith is wise in ruling.
  Caesar preserves his name because of his deeds,
Conquering all things, the hand proclaims the meaning of his
      name.
For him it is rest to have no rest, for him it is labor
  To be without labor. His passion is to suffer no passion.
When he is absent fear of him conquers: his fame enhances
  His name, his name fights his battles.
The arrival itself of Caesar contends on his behalf;
  The shadow of the name carries the weapons of an armed
      soldier.
Stern, indomitable, warlike, he strikes, siezes, impels enemies,
  Wars on criminals with his sword, his strength and his fear.
Bold, fearless and upright, he imbues, increases and fills
  His arms, his honor, and his face with blood, battle and
      threats.
He conceives, summons, posts a sentinal, is tireless, urgent in
      hope;
  In doubts he fights with the sword of certainty.

Valor, fame and confidence supply, aim and inform his
            strength,
    His courage, his mind with vigor, praise and conviction.
With this price Rome served him under the law of tribute,
    Having dared to recognize an eminence greater than its own.

52.   Eloquence ennobles and perception celebrates Ulysses,
        Grace of character is his name, fame makes him happy.
    In speech wily Ulysses abounds in the niceties of language,
        Has foresight is his perception and is powerful in cunning.
    An Ithacan, excelling in genius, a preserver of integrity,
        Vigorous of mind, provident in speech, powerful in skill
    To keep the nobility of his mind from languishing, his
        Living eloquence enhances and rekindles what is
                possibly lesser.
    Lest his eloquent utterance be widowed of feeling, the
        Nobility of his inner feeling weds itself to his tongue.
    He allies endowment with interest, and the joined fruit of
        Seed labors to fructify unto the harvest.
    With perception directing, ability conceives, and as teacher,
        Reason discerns, and good sense fosters.
    Talent sows the seed, study cultivates, practice aids sowing,
        Reason brings forth the tongue in service of its utterances.
    Perception running before and reason walking before
        Make the tongue heir of their teaching.
    The memory cells of Ulysses' head are not empty. The first
        Holds the designation of office, as the second and what
                follows.
    The first grasps, the next judges, the last ties down.
        The first plants, the second cultivates, the third reaps.
    The first conveys the subject matter, the second savors it,
            the third concludes it.
        The first serves help to the others; there are first doors,
    Then the hall and finally the home.
        The first and the second enclose the one that follows,
    Judges, wards off things that get in the way, are seen,
        And fends off disinclination and aversion by the door and bolt
                of good taste.
    The apex of reason abides within and greets
        The doors of the front and the bolt of the rear.
    It exceeds nature in power and the inner man is the
        Trusted teacher of the outer man.
    It exceeds the nobility of ministering discernment, surpasses
        Man's character and dominates weak nature.
    Wisdom deliberates on puzzling circumstances, and in the
        Judging balance it weighs the work just or wicked.
    The hand, friendly helper of the consulted mind, proceeds
        To act only after consulting the scales of justice.

To allotted destinies it confers adversity and makes
    The facts correspond to its words. It delivers
The intention to the adjoined act; the hand expressive
    Of the mind, matches one's words.
Age of mind does not impoverish virtues, but rather
    A youthful exterior exhales an adult fragrance.
He tempers his age with virtue; his greying youth
    Smacks of an elder with inner counsel.
By virtue he surpasses the desires of youth;
    By nobilities of mind he transcends the laws of his age,
The maturing of mind holds chastening reins on his age,
    And the mind is stunned that the mellow days arrive too
        soon.
Arrogance does not deflower the bloom of his mind;
    No taint smothers the charm of his great nobility.
Nor does fortune oppress the courageous;
    She, double in nature, finds him single in purpose.
Changeable, she finds him firm. Fickle, she finds him stable.
    Neither Antiphates,[52] nor Circe nor Charybdis can enfeeble
The stature of Ulysses' spirit. The brave, prudent
    And virtuous man conquers, nourishes, and brings to
Perfection the difficult, the just, the trustworthy.
    The eloqbent, prudent and generous man makes happy,
Embellishes and brings honor to his affections, his words,
    Dexterity of mind, beauty, generosity.
In eloquence, Tullius; in battle, Caesar; an Adrastus
    In counsel; in mind, Nestor, in strictness, Cato.

53.   Davus[53] is a scurilous vagrant, a gnawing parasite, an
        outcast
    Of the people, a disgrace to the world, a sickening plague;
An instigator of crime, the world's refuse, the ruin of
    Justice, assailant of the law, potent in deceit;
The source of idleness, barren of truth, overflowing with
    Trifles, deformed in body, pernicious in mind.
He is a Thersites[54] in shape, an Argus[55] for fraud, Tiresias[56]
    For justice, a Verres[57] in crime, Sinon[58] in deceit.
He is ignorant of virtue and struggles for vice; hostile
    To nature, he condemns the just, persecutes the virtuous.

---

[52] King of the Laestrygones who devoured one of Ulysses' companions and sank the Greek fleet returning from Troy. Cf. *Odyssey* X. 106 ff. and Ovid. *Met.* XIV 233 ff.

[53] A slave; cf. note 41.

[54] A Greek before Troy famous for his ugliness; cf. Ovid, *Met.* XIII. 233 ff.

[55] The guardian of Io said to have had one hundred eyes; cf. Ovid., *Met.* I. 625 ff.

[56] Famous blind soothsayer of Thebes; cf. Horace, *Sat.* II. 5.

[57] Governor of Sicily whose extortions and exactions became notorious through the celebrated orations of Cicero; cf. *Verres*, II. 3. 49.

[58] Persuaded the Trojans to accept the wooden horse; cf. Virgil, *Aeneid*, II. 79 ff.

Culpably he directs a destructive talent to harmful practices.
　　He claims he is completely the home of vice.
Crime is native to the slave, all deceit flows together in a unity.
　　He claims that all crime is his property.
He is inclined to cunning, blind to what is fitting and quick
　　　　to wrath.
　　He thinks he fails in self-service if he is not inflicting harm.
He lives for what is illicit, is the confusion of peace,
　　The cleaving of love; he is zealous to become bad, worse,
　　　　worst.
He slips here and there oozing with rumors, overflowing with
　　　　trifles,
　　And he covers good deeds and delates those best concealed.
Vessel of evil, pit of vices, filled with gall, he knows not how
　　To be unknowning of his villainy.
His mind full of evil knows not how to be ignorant of vice,
　　And the hand can be the teacher of sin.
For the habitue it is difficult to lose acquaintance with vice.
　　Culpably he tends toward the accustomed course of crime.
Unvaried practices become a representation of nature,
　　And he can be, as it were, the son of inequity.
Davus cannot but be harmful — he is born to be harmful.
　　If he cannot be harmful, he thinks he is degenerate;
The one devoid of trust and of duty, who suffers from deceit,
　　Who flies to things forbidden, who lack fidelity;
For his honorability is to lack honor, the one for whom
　　　　constancy
　　Is to be inconstant, his faithfulness is to have been faithless;
Villainy is to avoid crime, wickedness to avoid vice, and
　　Shamefulness to have felt shame for crime.
Fear makes him a hare, pillage a lion, a tail a he-goat,
　　Furtiveness a fox, ravage a wolf.
When he guides reason goes begging, when he directs
　　Virtue is exiled, and fidelity grows ill and dies.
Under his aegis virtue turns its back to evil, peace to rage,
　　Piety to wickness, faithfulness to treachery.
The tone used with the vocative case alone spares Davus;
　　There the unspoken word is silent.
Davus is a unique pollution of the air, deserving of chains,
　　Deserving of Jove's three-pronged bolt, deserving of death.
He repays adulation with threats, good with destruction,
　　Gifts with theft, honesty with deceit.
Behold the mountain of evil, his mind is vicious, his
　　Body profane, his speech deceptive, his hand heinous.
The harmony between kernel and husk denies he is a hypocrite.
　　Container and content are infected with like plague, similar
　　　　corruption.
Metonymy brings it about in Davus that of himself he not
　　　　endure

The same sins even though he has the same filth within and
    without.
When he sees it laughter causes sorrow.
    Laughter doles out pain and the outcome is sad with
        prosperity.
He is a clod of excrement, nature's disgrace, a burden
    to the earth,
    A glutton at the table, a disgusting house of dung.
He burns with the stings of envy, his soiled mind signals an
        appearance it adores;
    The filth of his mind moves into his face.
He runs here and there to dinners; after banqueting his belly's
    Friend is sluggish, consumes the fatty, spurns vegetables.
He is not evil, but born to destroy earth's products, he creates
    A sad evil that is not numbered in a ranking.
Cups are drained at his coming; the table is needy and begs
    For food, flagons, for wine.
Whose belly is his god, the kitchen his temple, the cook
    His priest, the fumes savor of Sabean incense.
He sits near the platter and imprisons the miserable food
    From which the hand, friend of the swollen belly, burgeons.
His concern is bowls and dishes. The roar of the belch and
    The rasping clarion of his belly bellow from both ends.
Bloated with food the heap creates winds and Davus can be
        an Eolus.
    Davus gapes sickly; with whirling winds bursting
Their prison, he gives out with what he cannot hold back.
    He tends toward lewdness; sick lust excites the
Two-pound brothers and all other members are warm, the male
        organ is rigid.
    The first syllable of the dactyl enters, the short syllables
Shatter the filthy ramparts with repeated thrust.
    By wickedness he proclaims servile madness and by his act
He brings into the open the slave's burden. He presses
    Upon charming backs, rages against the freeborn's backs,
He seizes the way of rebellious nature in forbidden bounds.
    He embues the innocent with corruption, the disease
Of his sick soul breaks up and flows into many.
    He is a sack of wickedness, a cloud to light, a storm
In the marketplace, a cruel pestilence, a swirling eddy.
    Full of harm, sick, indolent, he changes, destroys, represses
Joys, justice and good men with discord, fraud and deceit.
    Bare and destitute, empty of value in virtue, he rejoices
In a contest of honesty; in madness, fidelty — he abounds in
        one, he lacks in one.
    He chooses, desires, loves, distorts, rejects,
Admires quarrels, indecency, deceptions, alliances, temples,
        wickedness.
    At his birth virtue found its enemy and said:
"I see wars for myself, wars being prepared."

54. [59] First comes a rough draft which in its prosaic
   Measures limps to the ears of a wise judge.
Diligence, the condition and friend of the writer,
   Improves the rough draft and redeems what might be paltry.
Being in meter itself gives pleasure, but the value
   Of the material pursued will improve the final creation.
Hail, teacher, reflection of the fatherland, glory of the world,
   Exemplar of virtue, the fire of zeal, the way to honor.
Be not, I ask, unmindful of the mindful: I give thanks
   Like a vase to the potter, a rivulet to the spring, a
      wave to the sea.
I rejoice at the praise honor speaks for you, that fame is
      gathered about you,
   Because you shine with virtue, because you lead in reason.
You who makes wisdom contemptuous of men,
   Who is subject to the praises of even an envious judge,
You stand above all men in character; you the goal
   Of excellence in judgement surpass sickly nature.
I seek for the sight of you, languishing I desire you as a
   Healer; as a shipwrecked man, I desire your haven, as one in
      hell desires water.
Hail, mirror of the city and the world, remember your
   Suppliant pupil. The mind recalls the words of old.
When one is first born, reason looking at its pupil says,
   "I see my kingdoms, kingdoms are prepared for me."
I fall silent, the brevity of my meters shall bring this to
      a close,
   For the poem is awry which lacks brevity.

55. Marcia outshines in virtue's gifts, overflows in charm
   Of character, leads the way in sanctity.
She promotes womanly grace by her example, is without
   Arrogance, could not think of unchastity, is untainted with
      deceit.
She reflects her many gifts, modest in words,
   Cautious in counsel, vigorous of mind.
She subdues carnal urges, strives to transcend nature,
   And to be unconscious of her sex. She puts firmness
In the softness of her sex, rejects feminine deceits
   And displays understanding and radiates trustworthiness.
Graciousness of character pays visits to a frail nature.
   This courageous woman puts off innate evil. She is women
Not in fact, but in name. Her mind eschews the label of nature
   And empties it of deceit. The honesty of her speech portends
The value of her virtue, her countenance can announce her
   Honorable intention. No levity of mind suggests itself

---

[59] It is difficult to explain this passage among Matthew's descriptive examples. Faral's explanation seems untenable; cf. *Les Arts Poétiques,* p. 127.

As the fake origin of modesty, rectitude demonstrates itself
    By a matronly countenance. Her full brows and her
Modesty of mind display signs revealing a holy mind.
    The goodwill of her gaze is not a craving for Venus' sport.
Lewdness is not suggested in her movements.
    Marcia is strong in mind, makes vice her captive and makes
Sick sex desert itself for the better. Her buoyancy gives the
    Lie to sex, and the harmful husk disguises a kernel's savor.
The virulence of the vessel exhales the honorability of virtue;
    The odor of honey springs from the bark of the yew.
The yew yields honey and the hemlock smells of honey
    When resolute faith resides in a frail breast.
Things have changed: winter grows green,
    The crow turns white, vinegar gives nectar, the
Yew gives honey, the tamarisk, roses.
    Marcia embellishes the feminine sex, given honor to nature,
Makes the yew give honey. She chides her instinctive
    Wickedness, and the apathy of her sex
Does not relegate splendor of spirit into exile.
    The superiority of the kernel disputes with the husk;
The deficient exterior with the inner honeycomb.
    Marcia lacks guile, is virtuous, chaste, modest, is astounded
At reconciling sex with opposite goods.
    So many are the qualities fortified by patience, the guardian,
The nurturer of character, delightful partner of virtue.
    The upright woman to the upright man, sacred to the sacred,
Worthy of Cato, even before burial she merited the title:
    "Marcia, wife of Cato."[60]

56. The gifts of nature, the artist, are impoverished by the
           charm
    Of the daughter of Tyndareus, the blossoming of figure,
        the beauty of face.
Her appearance, lavish in beauty and shining with heaven's
    Gifts, scorns the human's face.
It is possible that her beauty, conscious of no equal, the
    Herald of hate, earned the praise of the judge of jealousy.
Her locks, not held by guiding knot, are the answer to gold.
    Permitted to extend its radiance to the shoulders,
It expands its beauty, the more pleasing outspread.
    Her brow tabulates, as it were, friendly words,
And unmindful of wickedness and lacking flaw, it entices stares.
    A milky way divides her dark eyebrows; the separated arches
Do not allow the hairs to run rampant.
    Her eyes outshining the stars with an approving naturalness,

---

[60] Cf. Lucan, *Phars.* II. 343.

Suggests they are the aides of Venus.
  In her face red mingling with allying white campaigns
And seeks tribute from rose's bloom.
  Nor like a stranger does color abide in her features,
Nor does regality fade from her face,
  The red and snowy-white countenance contrast.
The contour of her nose does not presume to be
  Too flat or be unfittingly large.
The enchantment of her rose mouth pants for kisses:
  Her delicate lips guided by a law of modesty smile fully.
Lest they float languid, the delicate lips are controlled in a
  Modest swelling and are formed with the honey of Venus.
Her teeth compete with ivory; held in orderly row
  They are eager to stand evenly in rank.
The smooth neck tries to outshine the snow, the dainty breast
  Chides its swelling, lying modest on her chest.

57. Or, if your listener is fastidious and says there is no merit in verbosity, let him get a physical description like this:

Her teeth resemble ivory, her noble forehead like milk,
  Her neck like snow, eyes like stars, lips like roses.
Her sides narrow at her waist up to the place where
  The lucious little belly rises.
The abode of modesty makes festive adjoining areas,
  Friend of nature and sweet home of Venus.
The sweetness of savor that lies hid in the realm of Venus
  The judging touch can fortell.
Her foot is small, limbs straight, legs full and
  Her hand does not shake with flabby flesh.
Lest her appearance lack full force, her endowments are
  Wed to her physical gifts: a good in representation.
The preciousness of matter, the superiority of figure
  Happily reflect on and enrich all members.
The surpassingly sweet production endows its matter;
  The beauty given substance concurs with the value
        of the matter.
The value of the flower does not droop in the wind of pride
  As the thorn with pity guards the tender rose.
She contributes to loving; such are my choices.
  The one from Vendome describes such as he loves.
With such preciousness were the Trojans wounded by the
        daughter of Leda,
  The booty of Paris, the fall of princes, the burning of Troy.
If the Greeks ask why the son of Priam abducted Helen,
  Set down a Hyppolytus there, he will become a Priapus.[61]

---

[61] Greek god of fertility.

58.   Beroe is a disease of nature, inky dregs,
　　　Uncouth in feature, the yield of tasteless nature,
The second Tisiphone, a public disorder, resembling a ghost,
　　　Vile in appearance, burdened with corruption,
Terrible in figure, foul to touch; the mange
　　　On her neck forbids her hands a rest.
When her mange lies hidden in protection by a stiff fur cap,
　　　The fly grieves at being deprived of its owed meal.
Her head is bare of hair and skin; a rust hardens ominously
　　　On her forehead, ugly, lurid, dripping with filth.
The rough forest of her brows protrudes forward,
　　　Strains the filth, bars the way with a bushy barrier.
Her gloomy eyebrows labor to contain the disease of her
　　　Neck and moves to cover her nostrils.
Her ear flows with filth. Unrounded they swarm with worms;
　　　Obese and dripping, they flop here and there.
Her eyes are livid, rheum plunges, the flood streams,
　　　Rules over bleary eyes, fills them with corruption.
While the starving flies flit about their food,
　　　Her lashes constantly enclose and trap them.
Her nose lying flat, stinking, warped with a
　　　Twisted canal, vomits lethal gusts.
Close by her drenched lips overflow and excreting scum
　　　Retreats to the diseased lodging of the nose.
Her vile and deformed cheeks, rigid with wrinkles, have
　　　Become crusted with blotches polluted by the eyes'
　　　　　putrid flow.
Her drooping lips are pale and faded; stinking spittle
　　　Oozing from a Cerberian mouth fouls her bosom.
Her teeth decay ravages, and ill breath and maggots
　　　Strike in a double devastation.
Nearby mange spares not her neck, crusty with pimples,
　　　Defiled with sores, drowning in corruption.
Her bosom is marked off by veins, and her shaggy skin,
　　　Matching bladders, counterfeit breasts.
A murky skinniness appears to rise over her ribs;
　　　Her skin grumbles that her thighs are fleshless.
Her belly looms with lust, stimulated by Lethe
　　　Close by, the door of hell, sad Chaos.
The woe of a pernicious hunch lessens her stature,
　　　And its marking begets a swelling back.
Her hollow trap gapes with numberless hairs,
　　　The flow of sulphurous whirlpool is red.
The descent to the flank bristles with briars;
　　　Cerberus howls; the gaping hollow spouts forth dregs.
The knee joint is unyielding, and drowned in the flowing flood,
　　　It whines they are smeared by Phlegethon.
The skin is infested with sores,
　　　And gout gnarls the digits of hands and feet.

59. Summary of What is Prescribed Above. Of the foregoing descriptions it is clear that with a majority, namely five, the purpose is to praise, while fewer, namely two, follow with blame. For theoretical instruction expressing blame ought to be somewhat less, since to it the consensus of human frailty is more inclined.

60. Reminder. The intelligence of the listener would be more eager to entrust things to its faithful memory, so that in the foregoing descriptions it comprehend general knowledge through specific names, lest it presume an understanding diverse from the intention of the author and singular to itself. For indeed what is to be considered carefully is not the effect of the utterance, but rather the intention of the one making it. So, to keep the special name from outweighing the other individuals of the same circumstance, age, dignity, office or sex, let what is said about the Supreme Pontiff, Caesar or other individuals who follow, be understood as attributed so that the special name, taking the place of the general name, calls to mind what is relevant. The special designation of a general subject ought to substitute for the nature of the subject not its material. **61.** Ovid has an example:

> I shall be called the Tiphys and Automedon of love.[62]

And Virgil:

> If I had some tiny Aeneas playing in my hall.[63]

For these proper names take the place of general names. **62.** And thus there are certain epithets which can be attributed one by one to the meanings of those preceeding names: as the power of binding and loosening can be attributed to the Supreme Pontiff, to Caesar, the stretching of a march to forbidden limits and the longing for conflict with prayerful desire; thus in Lucan:

> He preferred to burst through gates,
> Rather than find them open.[64]

And likewise for other characters.

63. Concerning the Description of a Person. Further, in the same description there should be many components. For some characters cannot be sufficiently labeled with one, two or more epithets. For just as it profits little to have an extraordinary rose choked by numerous thorns, and a unique pearl hidden in extensive bogs, so too, it does not suffice that one or a few virtues be assigned in praise of a person, when it may be that his store of vices is rather rich. Therefore a person also should for acceptance be given form with many epithets so that many will succeed where a single one cannot.

---

[62] *Ars.* I. 8.
[63] *Aen.* IV. 328.
[64] *Phars.* II. 443.

64. On Epithets. To continue, there are certain epithets which ought to be limited when applied to certain characters. There are others which ought to be amplified when applied to most characters; there are others which ought to be ascribed to everyone.

65. For example, in an ecclesiastical pastor, firmness of faith, longing for virtue, perfect religious zeal and the charm of fidelity ought to be enlarged upon; justice, indeed, should be played down lest, because of the sternness of his justice the church pastor appear to change into a tyrant: For his characteristic is

To spare the humble and war against the proud.[65]

66. On the other hand, the stern administration of justice should be ascribed with addition to a prince or an emperor, since weakness of justice is assigned with some detriment: As in Lucan:

Let him leave the court who wishes to be virtuous.[66]

Nor is what was said above about Caesar excessive:[67]

The imperial ruler
Neither exiles the arts nor routs studies.

We read that two verses made the following striking point about the idols which at Rome claimed for themselves the reverence due to the gods: as follows:

To be a god lacks reason if substance
Is stone shaped by human hands.

67. To Give Approval to the Form of a Woman. Further, the giving of approval to the form of the feminine sex ought to be amplified, but it ought to be restrained in the masculine sex. Whence in Ovid:

A less attended-to form becomes the male.[68]

In another place:

A virile form loves to be honored in moderate bounds.[69]

---

[65] Aen. VI. 853.

[66] *Phars.* VIII. 494.

[67] Cf. 51. v. 25.

[68] *Ars.* I. 509.

[69] *Her.* IV. 76.

68. Unless now or then a versifier describes the elegance of a boyish form for the greater clarity of his work, as Statius did in the *Thebaid,* who described a Parthenopean as marked with such an image of beauty, that when the beauty of his form was heard it was more easily possible for the listeners' adversaries to bewail the death of the boy. Hence Statius:

> The Arcadian wept for by both hosts alike.[70]

Here is a form that is elegant with a suitable joining of members and a pleasing complexion. —**69.** Again, to a matron one should ascribe stern severity, the lack of petulence, a fleeing from incontinence or lust. Lust is a cheap and vile thing coming from a cheap and vile stirring of members, and its longing is full of apprehension, a satiety full of remorse. —**70.** Likewise, the other characteristics which have to do with diversity of persons should be observed and assigned in a diverse way, that is to say, "Let each subject, having fittingly obtained its allotment, hold on to it." [71]

71. There are some epithets which can be applied with approval to any person of the masculine sex, such as solidity of manhood which weighed on the balance is indifferent to prosperity and adversity, for he is a real man who is forearmed and fights against ambiguous turns of fortune with constancy of mind, and similarly with patience which lends itself to preserving virtue: as Prudentius says:

> For that virtue is hollow which patience does not preserve.[72]

Or also Cato:

> Patience is the greatest of personal manners.[73]

72. On the Inflexibility of Material. Further, where two or more verses in the foregoing descriptions have the same meaning, let it be understood the statement was not made frivolously but selectively and for the avoidance of error and the choice of a remedy.

73. Because the main exercise of poetic talent consists of descriptive skill, in this section my advice will be that if anything is to be described, when articulating the description let the greatest support for credibility be presented: that the truth be said or what is probable, according to this passage from Horace:

---

[70] *Theb.* XII. 807.

[71] *Ars Poet.* 92.

[72] *Psychomachia,* V. 177.

[73] *Dist.* I. 38. *Catonis Disticha,* moral axioms written in verse form, is thought to be a spurious imitation of Cato.

Either follow tradition or create things that are self-consistant.[74]

Just as Lucan who so describes Curio, because he could easily suggest a desire for civil war by saying:

> Curio of the reckless heart and venal tongue was a
> Companion, once the voice of the people, and bold enough
> To champion and to mingle armed chiefs with the rank and
>   file.[75]

Similarly he so described Cato, who did not hesitate to undergo the crisis of death, lest, reduced to servitude to Caesar, the prize of his valor be begged for, when saying:

> For the state he became a husband and father;
> He worshipped justice and unswervingly preserved his honor,
> Bringing good to the commonwealth.[76]

74. About Intrinsic and Extrinsic Description. It should be noted that the description of any character can be twofold: one extrinsic, the other intrinsic; extrinsic when the exterior man or the beauty of his members is described; intrinsic when the characteristics of the interior man, namely, reason, fidelity, endurance, honorability, injuriousness, pride, excess and the other epithets of the interior man, that is, of the soul, are expressed for praise or blame.

75. Requisites in the Description of a Person. Again it should be noted that in describing a person according to the kind of office, or sex, or quality, or dignity, or condition, or age, the appearance should be especially delineated. Indeed, diversity of terms with identical meaning should not confuse the listener, so that he would take "character of deeds," "peculiarities," "epithets" and "personal attributes" as meaning the same thing. Because what is unique to any person has its place in the attributes of the person, I shall for greater clarity in this work go through them briefly and succinctly, so that the diligent listener in his own verses can assign more clearly condition or reasons drawn from the attributes of occupation or character. **76.** Indeed, here the terms "reasons" or "condition drawn from name or from nature" are to be understood differently from the discipline of logic. For in this work reason or condition drawn from name or nature are nothing but approving or rejecting something about the character by using an interpretation of name and the natural peculiarities, to lend uniqueness to the character or to remove it.

---

[74] *Ars. Poet.* 119.

[75] *Phars.* I. 269-71. Curio, Roman general and politician, died 53 B. C. He was an enemy of Caesar and friend of Cicero.

[76] *Phars.* II. 388-90.

77. The Number and Character of Personal Attributes.
Hence, there are eleven personal attributes: Name, nature, style of life, fortune, quality, diligence, reaction, deliberation, chance events, deeds, speech.

78. Reason or condition according to name occurs when, by interpretation of the name of a character something good or evil about the person is urged: as in Ovid:

Maximus, you who fulfill the measure of so great a name
And match your lineage in nobility of soul. . .[77]

And to cite my own example, one could choose reason or condition according to name, as we have said above in a description of Caesar:[78]

Caesar takes his name from his achievement, his hand
Cutting down all things explains the meaning of his name.

79. Example of an Attribute According to Nature.
There follows what nature says about the attribute. This attribute, however, according to Tullius, is divided into three parts, namely, into attributes derived form the body and those from the soul. **80.** From the body: as in Statius concerning Polynices:

Taller he was, with long stride and towering limbs.[79]

81. From the soul; as in the same author concerning Tydeus:

But neither with lesser strength
Did his spirit bear Tydeus and greater power instilled
Throughout his limbs held sway in a slight frame.[80]

82. Extrinsic attributes, however, are divided into those which are derived from one's race, fatherland, age, kindred or sex. There is a difference, however, between one's fatherland and race, because one's race is determined according to origin of its language; one's fatherland, according to its original locality. The reason is taken from a condition based on race, as in Virgil:

I fear the Greeks, even bearing gifts.[81]

---

[77] *Pont.* I. 2. 2.
[78] 51. v. 31-2.
[79] *Theb.* I. 414.
[80] *Theb.* I. 416-18.
[81] *Aen.* II. 49.

From Kindred, as in Statius:

> Cadmus, the origin of our fathers.[82]

From fatherland, as in the same author:

> The Martian land (Thebes)[83]

From age, as in Ovid:

> Let it be believed that she returned a virgin from a youth
> and one full of desire.[84]

From sex, as in Virgil:

> Come, break off with delays. Woman is always changing and
> inconstant.[85]

And so in Juvenal:

> The extravagent woman is not aware of means
> dwindling.[86]

The reason is taken from nature when "women" is said. In order to give examples of each one, one shall say:

> Though small of stature, Adrastus is strong with the
> Gifts of genius. The dignity of his mind reflects the man.[87]

The reason is taken from nature, with respect to soul, when one's "gifts of talent" are spoken of, from the body when the gifts of "small stature" are mentioned; from sex when man is mentioned: "As reflecting the man in dignity of his mind:" for this word "man" denotes age, strength, sex, and condition. From race as:

> The people of Gabbii grow with the acid of evil;
> The bitter contagion flows into the vice of mind.

From fatherland as:

> Rome craves gold, loves those who give it,
> Without a giver Rome refuses to favor the accused.

From kindered as:

> Eteocles a baleful offspring reminds of Oedipus;
> And contracts a thirst for evil from his arrant father.

---

[82] *Theb.* I. 680.

[83] *Theb.* IV. 434.

[84] *Her.* V. 129.

[85] *Aen.* IV. 569.

[86] *Sat.* VI. 362.

[87] The sole survivor of the seven against Thebes.

From age as:

> Love, a pleasing guest in tender youth, does its service,
>   But in an old man, Venus is ridiculous.

83. An Example of Style of Life. Next comes style of life as when in Lucan, Caesar says of Pompey:

> To you accustomed to lick Sulla's sword.[88]

And in Statius, Eteocles says of Argia:

> Will the queen, accustomed to her father's luxury
> Be content with this house?[89]

And likewise as above concerning Davus:[90]

> For one accustomed to them, it is difficult to put off vices.

But this attribute is divided into the accustomed nurture and those persons from whom someone draws his nurture.

84. An Example Derived From Fortune. Next we will treat the attribute called fortune; from it the reasoning is drawn in this manner.

Juvenal:

> There is nothing more intolerable than a wealthy woman.[91]

The reasoning from fortune occurs when "wealthy" is used. In Ovid:

> The uttermost misery is safe,
> For it lacks fear of an outcome still worse.[92]

Juvenal:

> The empty-handed traveler will face the robber with a song.[93]

Horace:

> Rare is eloquence in thin rags.[94]

Statius:

> It is pleasant for the miserable to speak and to
>   recall the sorrows of old.[95]

---

[88] *Phars.* I. 330.
[89] *Theb.* II. 438.
[90] *53. v. 25.*
[91] *Sat.* VI. 461.
[92] *Pont.* II. 2. 31.
[93] *Sat.* X. 22.
[94] As Faral notes this text is from Juvenal, *Sat.* VII. 145.
[95] *Theb.* V. 48.

To be safe, to grace the robber with a song, to discourse rarely, and to complain of one's misery are characteristic of both the poor and the distressed and concern fortune. Likewise earlier I spoke of Davus: [96]

Wickedness proclaims a servile madness.

For slavery and freedom are contained under fortune.

85. An Example Derived from Quality. From this source reasoning is thus drawn from appearance. From Ovid:

Though Ulysses was not handsome, he was eloquent.[97]

And again:

Typhis was master of the Haemonian ship.[98]

To give a characteristic form as a result of long application of mind pertains to habits of life, as being eloquent, a leader, honorable or skillful. And similarly it was said above about Ulysses: [99]

An Ithacan, he is superior in talent, a preserver of
Integrity, vigorous of mind, provident in word, powerful
in skill.

When "superior in talent" is mentioned, it is a reasoning drawn from nature; when "preserver of integrity" follows, the reasoning is taken from quality; "vigorous of mind" is a reasoning from nature; where it is said "provident in word" the reasoning is from speech; where "powerful in skill" is mentioned the reasoning again is from quality. And similarly in the other verses personal attributes can be assigned.

86. An Example Derived from Diligence. What follows concerns that attribute which is called diligence. Diligence is the strongly-willed and vigorous application of the mind to something to be done. From this is evolved the reasoning thus: Statius: [100]

They desire to trade life for praise.

Horace:

With shifting diligence, a man's age and spirit
Seeks influence and friendships, is a slave to ambition.[101]

---

[96] 53. v. 48.

[97] *Ars.* II. 123.

[98] *Ars. I. 6.*

[99] 52. v. 5.

[100] Cf. Faral's note pointing out that this passage is from Virgil, *Aen.* V. 230.

[101] *Ars. Poet.* 166-67.

The same author about Volteius Mena:

> He dies amid his diligence and grows old from
>   a desire for possessions.[102]

And similarly in the above passage about Caesar:[103]

> He sighs for a soldier's work.

87. An Example Derived from Reaction.

The following concerns reaction. Reaction is a sudden and fleeting change of spirit or body. The reasoning is evolved in this way. In Ovid:

> O how difficult it is not to betray guilt in your face.[104]

The same author in another place:

>   above all things the face
> Of the good man comes forward; [105]

Statius in the *Achilleid:*

>   O how much joy enhances
> One's beauty.[106]

In Lucan:

>   The spiritless crowd cowered before his fierce and
> Menacing words.[107]

Similarly it could be said of a boy and a timid virgin:

> Deep fear ravishes the countenance, and pallor
>   Unjustly makes itself heir of the ejected ruddiness.

Or thus:

> Color is the messenger of the mind and the prophet
>   Of the expression; inference is clearly expository of evil.

For joy and fear and pallor and life-style pertain to reaction.

88. An Example Derived from Deliberation.

What follows concerns deliberation. Deliberation is discernment in the scale of justice. It is a well thought out discrimination leading to rejection or acceptance. Therefore the reasoning is drawn in this manner. In Lucan: Brutus to Cato:

---

[102] *Ep.* I. 7. 85; Mena is a name taken from the Greek Menodorous. A freedman, he assumed the Roman gentile name Volteius from his patron (*Ep.* I. 7. 55).
[103] 51. v. 7.
[104] *Met.* II. 447.
[105] *Met.* VIII. 677.
[106] I. 167.
[107] *Phars.* V. 364; Adrastus, a king of Argos and leader of the expedition of "Seven Against Thebes."

> Do you therefore keep me erect when I am wavering,
> Give strength to my uncertainty with your sure strength.[108]

as if to say: "You who are able, give your counsel to me who nods."
Statius concerning Adrastus speaking:

> As for us, grief shall not lack reason.[109]

And Claudian:

> And let consideration of honor control your mind.[110]

Likewise as in the above passage concerning Ulysses:[111]

> The hand, friendly helper of the consulted mind proceeds
> To act only after consulting the scales of justice.

89. What Chance Is. Chance is here the regular result of calamity through which something is established concerning a person. As in Lucan:

> They sought out the standards of Illium's troops,
> And their camps about to perish because of their portents,[112]

as if, with the same portents under which they had previously entered the conflict, that is, for the Trojan destruction, when indeed, they had suffered a like misfortune. The same author says in another place:

> Fortune sustains many who do harm, and the gods can
> Be angry only with the unfortunate.[113]

In Statius where Argia speaks to Adrastus:

> Grant war, O father, and look upon the humble state
> Of your son-in-law lying low, look too, father, on
> This offspring of an exile.[114]

In Ovid:

> Sordid booty can bring no good in the end.[115]

It will be possible to use here my own example:

> Scarcely does the wretched extricate himself,
> Scarcely does he come to any happy circumstance,
> Who is subdued by the winter of angry prosperity.

---

[108] *Phars.* II. 244-45.
[109] *Theb.* III. 393.
[110] VIII. 268.
[111] 52. v. 37.
[112] *Phars.* III. 211-12.
[113] *Phars.* III. 448-49.
[114] *Theb.* III. 696-98.
[115] *Amores,* I. 10. 48.

90. The Distinction Between Chance and Fortune. Indeed, a distinction should be made between chance and fortune. For chance is the result of some misfortune; it frequently befalls a person. Fortune is a state of life which someone acquires either from his own decision, or because of an accident of time, or from human stewardship: from one's own decision just as if someone might of his own prompting pretend to undergo a stricture of poverty so he might acquire some temporal gain; because of an accident of time, as if one, oppressed by war and conquered, falls into unfortunate poverty, or as victor he be elevated to some privilege; from human stewardship as if one be born the heir of some noble person or king; this does not pertain to nature but to human structuring. The difference between chance and fortune is that chance is fleeting and fortune is rather more permanent than superficial and more efficacious.

91. An Example from Deeds. The following concerns deeds. A deed is the customary activity of a person through which we learn something about him. As in Lucan where Caesar speaks:

> I have accomplished sufficient great deeds:
> I have tamed the Northern tribes; I have subdued
> Enemy arms through fear.[116]

Again in Lucan:

> Caesar zealous for war rejoices to have no passage
> Except by shedding blood.[117]

Similarly in the above passage about Caesar:[118]

> The constancy of Caesar flashes in battle, he resists
>   Opposition, shatters the mighty, tames the savage.

92. An Example from Speech. The following concerns speech. It is the cultivated manner of speaking through which something is established about a person. As in Lucan about Caesar:

> Though he wore a humble garb, he was artless in
> Speaking the language of a common man.[119]

And in Horace:

> All words in excess flow away from a full mind.[120]

---

[116] *Phars.* V. 660-62.

[117] *Phars.* II. 439-40

[118] 51. v. 1-2.

[119] *Phars.* V. 538-39.

[120] *Ars Poet.* 337.

In Ovid about Ulysses:

> Nor was grace absent in his eloquent speech.[121]

Likewise in the above passage about the Pope:[122]

> The Pope teaches what should be taught, forbids what
>   should be forbidden,
> Punishes the guilty, and bears a spiritual scepter.

93. Concerning Actions. What follows is about the attributes of actions. Action is a deed or utterance because of which a man or woman is brought into court as a defendant; just as he or she is called a person who is brought to court as defendant.[123] **94. The Number and Designation of Attributes of Actions.** Action has nine attributes, namely these: The summary of the action, the cause of the action, previous circumstances, concomitant action, and subsequent action, capability of doing the action, quality of the action, the time and the place.

95. Aspects of the Summary of the Deed. The summary of the deed is what Tullius calls "a brief picture of the complete action,"[124] that is, the name or definition of the deed itself. From this is the reasoning drawn in this manner. In Juvenal:

> Who would not confuse heaven with earth and sea with sky
> Were a thief to annoy Verres, or a murderer Milo?[125]

Or in Lucan where Caesar says:

> O conqueror of the world, my lot in life.[126]

Similarly in the verses above about Davus:[127]

> Davus is a scurilous vagrant, a gnawing parasite, an outcast
>   Of the people, a disgrace to the world, a sickening plague.

96. The Twofold Divison of Cause, Which is Divided into Impulsive and Deliberate Causes. What follows concerns the cause which is divided into two parts. For one of these causes is impulsive, the other is deliberate. **97.** A cause is impulsive when we are hurled into an action by a sudden movement of the soul. As in Ovid:

---

[121] *Meta.* XIII. 127.
[122] 50. v. 13-14.
[123] This passage reveals Matthew's habit of needless repetition.
[124] *De Inventione,* I. 37.
[125] *Sat.* II. 25-26.
[126] *Phars.* VII. 250.
[127] 53. v. 1-2.

Love made her bold.[128]

In Juvenal:

At your order, a hungry little Greek will mount to the sky.

For each of these is an impulsive cause, namely love and poverty. Similarly with Io and Jove who was forced to present Juno with a cow to remove suspicion:

He gives a calf. He does not give it because forced to:
    It is rather like robbery, since it is not given freely.[129]

98. Concerning Deliberative Cause.

98. Concerning Deliberative Cause. A deliberative cause is considered in the gaining of what is convenient and avoiding what is unpleasant; in seeking the convenient, as in Lucan:

Meanwhile Magnus, unaware the leader was captured,
Was preparing arms so that he might fortify his troops
            with additional strength.[130]

In Horace:

I shall seek poetry wrought from what is familiar,
So that anyone may have the same hope for himself.[131]

In avoiding what is inconvenient, as in Lucan:

Then Caesar, fearing his front lines might collapse,
Holds his troops in motion at an angle behind the standards.[132]

In Horace:

To keep it from happening that old men's parts be assigned
            to youths,
Or those of adults to boys, we will ever be concerned with
Circumstances that are suitable to age.[133]

Similarly a condition can be drawn from a deliberative cause in gaining what is convenient and avoiding what is unpleasant:

Lest love languish and so that the lover attains his beloved,
    He is careful to fulfill his vows with entreaties or gifts.

Avoiding the unpleasant is posited in "lest he languish in love," and gaining what is convenient is posited in "so that the lover attains his beloved." **99.** But it seems that since deliberative cause is prudent so also the attribute of an action would be an attribute of a person. To this we say that

---

[128] *Met.* IV. 96.
[129] *Sat.* III. 78.
[130] *Phars.* II. 526-27.
[131] *Ars. Poet.* 240-42.
[132] *Phars.* VII. 521-22.
[133] *Ars. Poet.* 176-78.

deliberative cause and prudence are distinct attributes. For prudence refers to a person's good sense, not that of an action. Cause indeed means a cause of an action, not a cause of a person. —**100. Concerning Attributes which are Ascribed Before the Fact, Concomitant with the Fact, and After the Fact.** We will now consider those attributes which apply *before the fact, during the fact* and *after the fact. Before the fact, during the fact,* and *after the fact* refer to some circumstances of the principal deed which are adjuncts of the deed either by preceding, or accompanying, or following the action. **101.** The reasoning is taken from that attribute which is called *before the fact,* as in Lucan:

> Already the blood has touch and defiled the swords of
>   Caesar.[134]

102. From that attribute which is called *during the fact,* as in the same author:

> Gaul's fury is pouring over the wintry Alps.[135]

From that attribute which is called *after the fact* as in the same author:

> What lands will be given, which our veterans can plow?
> What walls to shelter the weary?[136]

In Juvenal:

> The helmet donned late is sorry for battle.[137]

And this example of my own illustrates those three:

> The smile of love, coitus, conception in the womb,
>   These are a triple sign of violated virginity.

103. The reasoning is from that attribute which is called *before the fact* when "The smile of love" is mentioned; for the agreement of the mind is the precursor of passion. There is reasoning from that attribute which is called *during the fact* when "coitus" is mentioned. There is the reasoning from that attribute which is called *after the fact* when "conception in the womb" follows. **104. An Example of the Capability of Doing the Deed.** What follows concerns the capability of doing the deed which derives from supporting conditions. In Ovid:

> To beguile a trusting girl is a glory cheaply earned.[138]

---

[134] *Phars.* II. 536.

[135] *Phars.* II. 535.

[136] *Phars.* I. 344-45.

[137] *Sat.* I. 169.

[138] *Hmr.* II. 63.

Or thus:

> It is easy for the mind to be deceived that knows not
>   how to deceive;
>   Simplicity can be deceived because of its facile credulity.

105. An Example of the Manner or Quality of the Deed.

What follows concerns the manner or quality of the deed. From which the reasoning is drawn in this way. Horace about Homer:

> So well does he invent, so closely does he mix facts with
>   fiction,
> That the beginning does not conflict with the middle or
>   the middle with the end.[139]

Virgil in his *Bucolics:*

> Overcome by my singing, would he not be restoring to me
> The goat my pipe had won by its song.[140]

Lucan:

> Why do you keep the words of mankind from the blood
>   of Caesar?[141]

Similarly it can be said:

> Hasty credulity is damaging, the impetuous hand
>   Is used to having frail effects.

Whence in Ovid

> Every onset has difficult approaches.[142]

—106. Of Time. What follows concerns time. The reasoning is from time when from the suitability of time something is either proved or disproved inferentially about the action. As in Virgil's *Bucolics:*

> Now everything is in bloom; now is the most beautiful
>   time of the year.[143]

---

[139] *Ars Poet.* 151-52.

[140] III. 21-22.

[141] *Phars.* VII. 81

[142] *Rem.* 120.

[143] III. 57.

107. Likewise an example of my own can be used, such as, in restrained brevity we have description of the four seasons of the year, this way: [144]

Description of the four seasons of the year

Rosy spring plays with the tender flowers, it labors
    To decorate Rhea with more flowery hair.
Summer, the friend of the sun, burns, and bubbling with heat,
    Struggles to be a season with its own name.
Autumn is the vinedresser and cupbearer of Bacchus;
    It toasts the delights of the grapeclusters and fills the
        storehouse with harvest.
Winter bristles with its triple garments, the step-mother
    Of flowers, and the sad companion of a playful spirit.

108. The epithets of the four seasons of the year are thus described for brevity's sake:

The parts of the year are twice two: spring is warm,
    Summer burns, autumn gives wine, winter freezes.

Or thus:

Spring is the begetter of flowers, summer the nurturer of fruit.
    Autumn the vine-dresser, and then prodigal winter comes.
Lucifer flees the stars, the precursor of the rising sun.
    The day returns to breathe better with night in exile.
Aurora sends the darkness in exile,
    Deprives Tithomus of his bed and reddens the face of Jove.
Light steals along, accompanied by prickly frost,
    And a greyness strives to anticipate the moment of sunrise.
Phoebus dispenses his more abundant beams, his horses puff
    In running to divide the day.
The sharply decending chariot of Phoebus glides to the
        antipodes;
    With a slower wheel it sinks in the west.

—109. Place. The following concerns place. The matter is drawn from place when because of fitness of place it is inferred that something had been done or not done. In Horace:

Kindly Athens added somewhat more in the arts.[145]

---

[144] It is clear that Matthew considers description to be the primary object of verse writing. The following lengthy passages of *descriptio temporis* and *descriptio loci* inserted within his discussion of action reveals also that he pays lip service only when he says "I fall silent, the brevity of my meters shall bring this to a close, for the poem is awry which lacks brevity." See above 54. v. 23-24.

[145] *Ep.* II. 2. 43.

In Lucan:

> Curio rejoices as if the luck of place would do the warring.[146]

110. And it should be noted that, as was said about the descriptions examined above, a description of place or of time can very often be unnecessary, and very often can be appropriate. For unless we should wish to convey something to the listener by the help of time or place, the description will have to be omitted, as in this example from Cicero: Cicero against Verres,[147] when he was prosecuting Verres for having committed adultery in Sicily, described the many delights of that region, saying that the trees were marked with the gifts of spring and meadows painted with a variety of flowers, and crystal-clear fountains; so that having learned of the beauty of the place, the line of reasoning could infer that in a place shown him by Cicero of so great beauty, Verres had more readily committed adultery. **111.** To bring in an example of my own, the following can serve as a topography:

Description of place

> The place is an eager concern of nature, where abound
>   The delights of spring, its grace and plentitude.
> Nature flatters the place, prodigal in giving she
>   Can be in need of things given.
> Having transgressed moderation in giving and keeping nothing
>   for herself,
>   She bedecks royally the place with increased ornaments.
> The land is luxuriant with long grass, the grass....[148]
>   Brevity, friendly to the ear, comprises and gives pleasure.
> The waters are not infested by the heat of the sun,
>   Instead a row of bending branches preserves the moderate
>   warmth.
> Wedding its rights to friendship with the sun, the moisture
>   Resolves to nourish the foliage into flowers.
> There is yet a second gift; birds in the zeal of their garulous
>   Vocal chords heap beauty on beauty.
> Crying out "kill" grieving Philomena complains
>   And recites her hurts with pleasing sorrow.
> The voice of the blackbird echoes, when tamed it is accustomed
>   To be well-known for its corruption of human speech.
> The parrot ready to contribute to the triumphs of Caesar
>   Cries out with garbling tongue, "Farewell."

---

[146] *Phars.* IV. 661.

[147] Verres was brought to trial in 70 B.C. and was defended by Hortensius and prosecuted by Cicero. The trial resulted in his voluntary exile in Marseilles. Of the six orations against Verres composed by Cicero, only the first was actually delivered.

[148] See III. 32. v. 16-17 for some of the missing lines. Faral's note p. 148 explains the omitted passage.

Tereus is armed for strife and crime.[149]
   The cheerful lark with prophetic voice announces the day.
The peacock, with eyes like the stars of Argus, struts
   And glows with the beauty of ornamented vesture.
The sacred dove of Venus builds its nest with twigs,
   Paying the price of lewdness by wearing a simpler plumage.
The amorous turtledove, widowed of her first mate,
   Wails while loving the pledge of lasting love.
The quail, set off by her markings, lives and sings here,
   Along with the partridge fated to be racked on a strait spit.
The swan which announces its own obsequies, and looks down
   On the moment of it imminent death, leaps up from the pool.
The magpie pours out matter for conflict in logic;
   It conceals its members with some in-between color.
Here the king of little birds is present,[150] which gives to
   Its small stature honor according to the nobility of its name.
The woodpecker artificer is not absent; its beak is its tool:
   For itself or its fellows it digs hospitable roofs.
The noisy and avaricious jackdaw turns black and is given to
   Gracing our homes during its banishment.
The sparrow submits or pursues, unquieted Venus coursing
   In its loins, on which it drops names.
The crow and the raven are not here nor does the owl
   Defile the sacred place with its rasping groans.
The dominance of the eagle is lacking, for the dignity of
   His royal rank might rupture the songs of the commoners.
Thus when complaint urges the birds to an exchange of song,
   One would think he is hearing an orchestra.
The flowers give fragrance, the grass grows, the trees bear,
   Fruit overflows, the birds chatter, the river murmurs,
       the air is cool.
Birds please by voice, the grove by shade, the air by
       coolness,
   The fountain by drinking-water, by its murmur the
       stream, by its flowers the ground.
The murmur of water is charming, the voices of birds are
       harmonious,
   The smell of the flowers fragrant, the stream cool, the
       shade warm.
The beauty of the mentioned place feeds the five senses were
   You to note all the marked points together.
The water delights the touch, flavor the taste, the bird is
   The friend to the ear, and grace to sight, scent to the nose.
The elements are not absent: the earth conceives, the air
   Caresses, heat awakens, moisture nourishes.
A maiden, the masterpiece of a solicitious spirit, flatterer
   Of flowers, befriends the water of the mentioned fount.

---

[149] According to the myth, Tereus pursuing Procne and her sister with an ax for serving up the flesh of his son in a dish was changed into a hawk and they into a swallow and nightengale.
[150] The wren.

112. Some of the attributes action has are had in the performance of the act. Connected with the action are the summary of the action, its cause and the triple functioning, namely *before the fact, concomitant with the fact* and *after the fact.* The performance of the act contains four other attributes, namely as follows: the quality of the act, the capability of doing it, the time and the place. Two other kinds of attributes pertain to an action, namely, the adjuncts to the act and the consequence of the act, which should be passed over for the present, lest the prolixity of discourse bring dissatisfaction to the speech and weariness to the speaker.

113. If indeed, the attributes of action are time and place, because they are inseparable, they are attributes of action: for whatever happens, it happens in time and place. They ought to have been explained more fully: therefore I should not be reproached for the length of the above topography, which, since it has grown old from too much contact, I have inserted in a new little work so that the little crow, stripped of its stolen colors, might produce laughter.[151] For certain people, who think it glorious to live at another's table, have presumed to take unto themselves the verses of that topography.

114. Further, the number of examples did not go beyond the attributes of action and of persons so that if two or more examples be introduced, the first would be judged clear, the second clearer, and the third clearest. For the building is more durable for which a variety of columns forms a support. For a plentitude of example is beneficial to the one making examples. For even a mouse is more readily caught in the toils of a trap when his own single base offers him refuge.

115. Further, if in a single example a diversity of attributes occurs, reference must be made not to the execution of the speech but to the purpose of the speaker. For words bear the markings of the sense which creates them, not from that they create. As in this example cited above:[152]

> Let it be believed that she returned a virgin from a
> youth and one full of desire.[153]

When "youth" is mentioned it is a reasoning from nature; when full of desire" is mentioned it is a reasoning from feeling; and similarly with many examples. Thus examples are to be referred to the purpose of the person making them.

---

[151] Horace, *Ep.* I. 3. 19-20.
[152] Cf. 82. v. 12.
[153] *Her.* V. 129.

116. Indeed the attributes both of action and of person, are brought together in this little verse:

Who, what, where, means, why, how, when.

Who contains eleven attributes of person; *what* contains the content of the act and the triple carrying out of the action, that is, *before the fact, during the fact* and *after the fact; where* contains place: *means,* the capability of doing the action; *why,* the cause of the action: *how,* the mode or quality: *when,* the time.

117. Reminder. Further, to keep the communication of the instruction from seeming to disagree with the teacher, in the above descriptions either *zeugma* or *hypozeuxis* can be ascribed almost everywhere, and also other colors or figures. We will speak more clearly about these figures in what follows. Indeed, in the verses presented above the careful listener should think over the method of speaying rather than the circumstances of what is said; thus, in the little work in hand the charm of what is proposed, not the seriousness of its presentation would be understood to have place.

118. Further, lest prolixity, the mother of boredom, presume to assault delicate ears, because "no one will be forced to keep my gift,"

Nor is there ever a lesser labor than that of having kept silent,

let the little rivulet of this present little work conclude on time. For very often the charm of a beautiful old song overflows into boredom in listening.

Lest my lyre act foolishly, I lapse into quiet; delay
Is the stepmother of approval. Part of the labor is used up,
      part survives.

Here the transition is used:

Sicilian Muses, let us sing of greater things.
    Depending on you, we unfurl full sails on the sea.[154]
The orchards do not please all nor the lowly tamarisks
      make us glad,
    Indeed, pleasing it is to share in the arrival of the laurel.[155]

The First Part Ends, The Second Begins.

---

[154] Virg. *Ecl.* IV. 1.
[155] Virg. *Ecl.* IV. 2.

[II. THE FORM OF WORDS]

1. Since in the above part of this work our pace tarried a little concerning the mode of describing, when we were about to go over to the three-fold beauty of versifying we judged it fitting to divulge an imaginary vision of the preceding night for the pleasure of the audience, so that with the help of a light presentation pleasing narrative might prevail, receptivity might be plentiful, attention refreshed, good will flourish, the audience echo in sound, the annoyance of boredom be averted, and the productive desire for learning be more richly fulfilled. **2.** For I seemed to see, in the excellent quiet of the preceding night, that after the barrier of wintry idleness had been broken, when Flora, the portress of spring, adorned royally the lap of the earth with a many-colored mantle of flowers, she instilled by drops the delights of her favor in the Areopagus[1] rather than in other places so that the intimate sweetness of the fragrance might offer both a relief from labor and nourishment for study for the students of the Areopagus, that is, so that after the surface of the earth was painted the sweetness of her savor, overflowing more fully, received through the vehicle of smell, at the abode of reason, whatever might fall asleep lulled by memory's ashes, a faithful tongue would be able to express more freely with the aid of a trusted memory. Hence, in the remaining places the teacher of student Flora producing his art in a spirit of avarice, as it were, while taking care about the elegance of the passage mentioned above, took a devious step in mediocrity and almost prodigally turned toward the parallel vice of extravagance. Indeed, in the mentioned place the delicate infancy of flowers in full abundance with dedicated desire longs for the beginnings of birth, and refusing to be contained longer in its cradles, strive to indulge in half-formed laughter.

---

[1] A low hill at Athens continuing westward the line of the Acropolis from which it is separated by a depression of the gound. Portions of the summit are hewn smooth to form platforms, probably for alters. It is known as the meeting place of the earliest aristocratic council. At the base of the steep rock on the northeast side is a deep and gloomy cleft holding a dark pool of water. This was the famous shrine of the furies.

3.   *Description of Nature*

> Here Genius struggles for the better, spring presents earth's
> Brilliant bosom with a mantle colored with grass.
> The infant blades swell, a balmy breeze summons the
>   splendor of spring;
> A tiny flower sparkles forth, the new-born rose fortells
>   of warmth.
> A lucid spring, one sweet as nector, quickens, nourishes,
>   gives growth
> To the blossoming meadows, the breath of fragrance.
> The hostile hardness of the foe does not despoil nor destroy
> The temperateness, and the flower, spring's friend, holds
>   it's splendor.

Description of Philosophy and her handmaidens

4. In the place of stated beauty Philosophy, surrounded by her hand-maidens, with beguiling zeal, so as to feed its labor on the myriad perfumes of the flowers, is pleased to lie very often upon the flowers, very often to meander.

5. Philosophy then, painted without artificial charms, seems to breathe out, as it were, by some special prerogative a divine reverence and to scorn by inferences of many kinds the fraility of human nature. A severe brow signals the inflexibility of matronly modesty; a spirited eyebrow indulges itself with no sign of petulance; the ardor of the eyes proceeding with direct and pentrating regard refuses to be turned away to secondary things. Lively complexioned cheeks banishing from itself the adultery of fashioned color, proclaims active living; alert lips touch another modestly, lest from too much talking they venture to wander, and such nobility makes its face beautiful, because from proper purpose of mind it proclaims activity; an appearance shaped from unfailing vitality is determined to disavow fragile nature. Her stature of indeterminate description cannot at all be defined in fixed terms. Her garments, as Boethius[2] asserts, perfected of delicate threads, with clever craft and lasting material—in revealing its character and attributes, human ingenuity becomes infirm, eloquence goes begging, and human discretion confesses itself to suffer offense. Indeed, while main-taining watch on school books it does not cease to bestow the joys of an elo-quent heart among the nourishing and servant arts.[3] **Concerning Tra-gedy.** Among these is tragedy shouting loudly with multifarious cries:

---

[2] Cf. his *Consolation of Philosophy*.
[3] The seven liberal arts.

Throwing aside his bombast and six-syllable words,[4]

and relying on buskined feet, with a fixed expression, with threatening brow she trumpets forth myriad signs of her customary fury.

6. Concerning Satire. Satire is near in the next seat, of meagre silence, her countenance prodigal of shame, with oblique eyes attesting to a mind askew, her lips spread with continuous prating; she presumes to keep so little of her sense of shame because she does not blush at all at her own nakedness.

7. Concerning Comedy. Thirdly, comedy slips in, with lasting humble character, with head bowed low presenting delights of no celebration.

8. Concerning Elegy. Fourthly,

Elegy sings of trembling loves,[5]

with approving brow, with eye, as it were, summoning, with a forehead revealing capriciousness, whose little lips are abundantly savory and seem to pant for kisses; she comes last not because of unworthiness, but rather from irregularity of measure. Nevertheless, in the creation of solace she compensates for the drawback of uneven proportions as in this passage in Ovid:

The fault in her measure will be the source of her charm.[6]

Indeed, these four dominate in metric mode when they strive by turns for the official epithet, because

Meter has no loyalty to its comrades and all power will
Be impatient of an equal.[7]

Elegy, I believe, makes known the three-fold elegance of skill in versifying. **9.** For there are three things which are detectable in verse; polished words, ornamented expression and inner charm.

---

[4] *Ars Poet.* 97.
[5] Ovid, *Rem.* 379.
[6] *Am.* III. 1. 10.
[7] Cf. Lucan, *Phars.* I. 92-93.

Concerning the Three-Fold Elegance of Versification. Verse gathers its elegance either from the beauty of the inner meaning or from the exterior ornamentation of words, or from the mode of expression.

10. From the beauty of inner meaning, as in Horace:

> It is profitable to go to a fixed point, if it is
>   impossible to go further.[8]

And again in Lucan:

> The sin of the many goes unpunished.[9]

For these examples have no elegance of ornaments in the verses, because words almost in daily use occur, nor is there any elegance from the quality of expression since neither figures nor tropes can be detected there; but the elegance derives from the general meaning, which in both examples is offered for our understanding so that the beauty of the things signified is judged to abound in the meaning itself.

11. Elegance in verses is derived from the surface ornament of words when the verse draws its beauty from the charm of its words and makes friends for itself of a more pleased audience, as in Lucan:

> every distinction lay hid under
> The cover of plebian garb.[10]

Again in the *Achilleid* of Statius:

> Emerging from Ocean, day rescued the world from dark
> Enfolding shadows,[11]

Indeed, on this point the versifier should be well prepared, lest from a poverty of ornaments a shaggy accumulation of words seems to go begging in meter; but by a particular comparison taken from material things, just as no one can weave a festive garment from goat's wool or old rags, because a little ferment can ruin the entire lot; so too in verses, if the material of the words is festive the ceremonial character will flow over into what is wrought, and measures lacking ornamentation will reveal either the ignorance or the negligence of the versifier. Indeed, as in the forming of a material object the whole material shines more beautifully because of the close positioning of some pearl or inlay; similarly, there are some expressions which are, as it were, substitutes for jewels; from skillful positioning of these the whole meter will seem to be celebrating. For multiform ornamentation of them imparts by positioning the benefit of its beauty to other expressions, and by association, as it were, applies the attractiveness of a certain festive character.

---

[8] *Ep.* I. 1. 32.
[9] *Phars.* V. 260.
[10] *Phars.* II. 18.
[11] II. 1-2.

12. Therefore, since every good gleams more brightly when applied to the commonweal, and since a hidden lamp is capable of nothing, to give shape to the youths' education I have inserted in this present work certain expressions which are mutually helpful in ornamenting as an example of the ways of arranging similar terms. Some of these expressions are adjectives, some are adverbs; however, substantive words are not completely excluded from the ornament of meter; but I give less emphasis to substantives and more to adjectives because the number of adjectives is greater. Nor is the expression verbal adjective meaningless: of these words some are substantives, some are vocatives, some are adjectives; for ornamentation of words is found more frequently in modifying nouns and verbs; for they are determinative of characteristics, in whose use the refinement of verse-making especially depends.

13. What and How Many Adjectives arc Used in Verse.
We must first treat adjectives: what kind of bond do they require in metrical arrangement through the movement of verse as also through exemplifying clauses. These expressions have various terminations. **14.** Some terminate in -*alis,* some in -*osus,* some in -*atus,* some in -*uus,* and some in -*aris.* There are also other endings for modifiers: but in the foregoing a more ornate embellishment of the words and a more elegant joining of words can be implanted.

15. Of these words, however, whose use is less frequent are found those adjectives ending in -*alis,* as *official (officialis), material (materialis), representative (effigialis), venal (venalis), superficial* (superficialis), *triumphal (triumphalis), favorable (favoralis), funereal (exsequialis), mysterious (mysterialis), imperial (imperialis), pontifical (pontificalis), solstitial (solstitialis), judicial (judicialis), initial (initialis), conjectural (conjecturalis), terminal (exitialis), unnatural (prodigialis), legal (legalis), connubial (connubialis), collateral (collateralis).* An example of the joining of these could be as follows:

Thus either for choice or avoidance:

	The herd is the *official* sign of a shepherd.
Further:	The *official* honor glorifies the cleric.
	Material possession increases respect.
Or thus:	An *imitative* honor is a pillager to comeliness.
	A *brilliant* depiction enriches matter.

16. An Example of the Word "Triumphal." There follows an
example of the word *triumphal,* which seems to accord with the inexperienced whose presumption anticipates knowledge, whose education is preceded by teaching; it is the unworthy mercenary who usurps the place of the archimandrite; the one unworthy of dependence tries to keep hold of absolute power; the one who though he bring a man to us with him, fell

from heaven like a third Cato; who perhaps knows how to make likenesses of the cypress:[12] who tries to build without a foundation, to work without material; about this man and those who suffer from such sickness, should I wish to give a sample of counseling, the supply renders me resourceless;[13] who under the pretense of superficial knowledge cloaks the blindness of deeper ignorance. **17.** Against them Horace inveighs saying:

> O you imitators, you servile herd...[14]

and later compares them to the unskilled Iarbitas who by imitating Timagenes[15] in oratorical power with bellowing declamation burst his diaphragm. hence in Horace:

> In imitating Timagenes, Iarbitas caused himself to burst
> > asunder,
> As he sought to be considered urbane and eloquent.[16]

18. By way of example we shall thus have to come down firm on these:

> The *borrowed* verses and *superficial* gem.
> *Triumphal* abundance is medicine to the wicked.

19. Further: Reputation delights the mob with *favorable* honor.
or: *Favorable* acceptance has a lofty name.
Further: The owl sounds the *funereal* signal of death.
Further: Verses give *perpetual* honor to the poet
Or: Box-wood gives a *mysterious* cloak to the cross.
Or: The priest sings the *mysterious* service.
Further: The citizen fears the *imperial* judgment.
Or;   *Imperial* love has a right against the gods.
Further: The *pontifical* hand holds the heavenly scepter.
Or: Popes wield a *pontifical* scepter.
Further: Sorrow makes every season *solstitial*.
Further: The dependant trembles at the *judicial* hearing.
Further: Eve was the *initial* seed of evil.
Or: Fear of God is the *initial* good.

(For the fear of the Lord is the beginning of wisdom.)

Further: The mind speaks through one's face and character;
> The prophet of sorrow exhibits *suggestive* signs with his
> > voice.

---

[12] Cf. *Ars Poet.* 19.

[13] Cf. Ovid. *Met.* III. 466.

[14] *Ep.* I. 19. 19.

[15] A rhetorician and an historian, was a native of Alexandria who later opened a school of rhetoric in Rome

[16] *Ep.* I. 19. 15.

The following can be examples of conbinations:

> *Unnatural* sin is a *fatal* evil.
> The *Connubial* rite is a *legal* union
> *Collateral* love is a blemish of form.

20. Adjectives Terminating in -osus.

What follows concerns adjectives ending in *-osus*. Because Apella the Jew would believe in authentic examples, we will have to proceed very often from authoritative examples and very often with those of our own making.[17]

	Believe me, giving is a *noble (ingenuosa)* thing.[18]
Or:	A virtue of the soul is a *noble (ingenuosa)* companion.
In Ovid:	And to the reluctant comes the *obliging (officiosa)* muse.[19]
Or:	A *helpful (officiosa)* hand serves the entire body.

Or in Claudian: *Demanding (imperiosa)* hunger is the nurturing discord of war.[20]

Or:	The *imperial (imperiosa)* majesty of rules flourishes.
Further:	*Delicate (deliciosus)* love changes matter.
Or:	*Delicate (deliciosa)* love pauperizes the resources of speech.
Or:	*Delicate (deliciosa)* hunger disdains the vegetable diet.
Further:	*Ambitious (ambitiosa)* thirst torments the craver.
Further:	The *talented (ingeniosa)* anxiety savors more fully.
Further:	Love in boys is an *impetuous (impetuosa)* contagion.
Further:	*Envious (invidiosa)* hunger is a virtue to me.
Further:	Trust in wickedness is an *unnatural (prodigiosa)* thing.
Further:	Superfluity produces *ragged (panniculosa)* verses.
Further:	*Suspicious (suspiciosa)* conjecture brings forth fear.
Further:	*Insidious (insidiosa)* fate works to change fidelity.
Further:	*Contentious (litigiosa)* chatter injures the lord.
Further:	Love of an old veteran is a *ridiculous (ridiculosus)* thing.

21. Adjectives Terminating in -atus.

The following concerns adjectives terminating in *-atus,* such as: *material (materiatus), circular (orbiculatus), partial (particulatus), articulate (articulatus), inveterate (inveteratus), inviolate (intermeratus), immediate (immediatus), immoderate (immoderatus),* unsatisfied *(insatiatus), inviolate (inviolatus), irrevocable (irrevocatus),* and participles of similar form as *entitled (intitulatus), beginning (primitiatus), unburied (intumulatus), entangled (illaqueatus), unviolated (inviolatus), contradicted (infitiatus), ornamented* (pharleratus), *unornamented* (enucleatus).

---

[17] Cf. Horace, *Sat.* I. 5. 100. In the Rome of Augustus the Jews were regarded as peculiarly superstitious.

[18] Ovid. *Am.* I. 8. 62.

[19] *Pont.* I. 120.

[20] III. 30.

Now these which follow are examples of combinations:

>   The value of the matter enhances *material* things.
> Further: A *circular* house is of the same color to the eyes.
> Further: *Partial* reasoning accepts increase.

(For *divided* knowledge is susceptible to growth.)

> Further: The *articulate* voice pleases the listeners.
> Further: An *inveterate* illness is difficult to cure.
> Further: May the *inviolate* mother come to our aid.
> Further: An *immediate* home pleases everyone.
> Or thus in closing: *Immoderate* love, *insatiate* hunger.
>   *Sacrificing* faith, *irrevocable* crowd.

22. Participles of this termination can also be numbered with adjectives of this kind. For every participle is an adjective and a derivative: an adjective in meaning, a derivative in origin. This then about them:

>   The *entitled* nobility of the king is a sign.
> Further: The *beginning* fruit of the sea's foam was Venus.
> Further: The precept was tottering, *unburied* piety is
>   flattened.
> Further: An *entangled* lover prepares for both right and
>   wrong.
> Or thus: An *entangled* lover does not fear what he ought to
>   fear.
> Further: *Inviolate* love tortures those who lust.
> Further: *Refuted* death results from a poor bite.
> Further: *Ornamented* fraud lies hidden under title of fidelity.
> Further: *Unornamented* fidelity flourishes in obedience.

23. Indeed, to this method in the following way very similar examples can be assigned, such as *amplified (amplificatus), notified (notificatus), vociferated (vociferatus), connected (continuatus), certified (certificatus);* and many like this can be assigned; because their metrical placing has been aired about by everybody, the blear-eyed and barbers,[21] examples of them must be omitted. For those utterances in which the versifier is crude are not to be treated, a sort of Neoptolemus,[22] "who now as a soldier comes for the first time into new conflict," and is too unprepared. For when the rather small knowledge of an attentive listener applies itself, the learning is more effective. And again, what travels successively into the ears of many banishes the appetite of the listener from itself. For

> The doctrine which everyone works with perishes; for it
> Usually slips into every kind of fault, which places the
>   people in thraldom.

---

[21] Cf. Horace, *Sat.* I. 7. 3; also Part I. 3.

[22] Also called Pyrrhus, son of Achilles, one of the heroes concealed in the wooden horse. He was fetched from his home by Ulysses, because it had been prophisied that he and Philoctetes were necessary for the capture of Troy.

24. Adjectives Terminating in -ivus. Now we take up the adjectives ending in *-ivus* such as *relative (relativus), vocative (vocativus), adoptive (adoptivus), expositive (expositivus), responsive (responsivus), continuous (continuativus), abusive (abusivus), incentive (incentivus), connective (conjunctivus), united (collativus), effective (effectivus), impulsive (impulsivus), negative (negativus), revived (redivivus), entreative (petetivus);* the following are examples:

> Just fidelity rejoices in *relative* honor.

(Indeed, as Ovid asserts:

> The common herd approves of friendships according to
> their usefulness) [23]

Or thus, concerning the conversation of lovers who are in the throes of passion:

> In the light of day with the exchange of words they
> contract for evil,
> The sun at rest, each shouts a *mutual* "farwell."

Further: The front page bears the *beckoning* words.
Further: Christ cherishes us with *adoptive* piety.
Or: The *expositive* tongue reflects its own feeling.

(For the mouth speaks from the fullness of the heart.)

Further: I arouse meters through *responsive* words.
Further: Love rejoices in a *continuous* pact.
Further: The holy assembly avoids an *abusive* charge.
Further: Honesty of face cloaks the *incentives* of an evil utterance.

(Though here, *incentive* is a substantive not an adjective.)

Further: A mistress lives for *continuous* union.
Further: A lawyer gathers contraries, and from combined
disagreement puts together a *collective* ranking.
Further: An *effective* cause imbues the holy work.

(For an effect must correspond to its cause.)

Further: An *impulsive* cause is tutor to an evil act.

(For necessity has no law.)

Further: Love is renewed by a *negative* voice.

(For as Ovid testifies,

> We always strive for what is forbidden and desire
> what has been denied; [24]

---

[23] *Pont.* II. 3.8.
[24] *Am.* III. 4. 17.

Hence he also adds:

> He sins less who is free to sin; the power
> Itself makes more languid the seeds of sin.) [25]

Further: Debaucheries are revealed with *entreative* zeal.

(Because, with Ovid as authority,

> chaste is she whom no one has asked.) [26]

Or thus: With an *entreative* voice a procurer urged Thais.

25. There are many words with this ending in the second application; hence because they cannot be used with substantives in the first application they change from their proper meaning to another. A scarcity of examples at this point can be more readily excused. And again many words with this ending are excluded from verse because of the inappropriateness of the lengths and the unsuitability of syllables, as for example, *indicative (indicativus)*, *deprecating* (deprecativus), and similar words.

26. Adjectives Terminating in -aris.
What follows concerns a few adjectives ending in *-aris*, such as *articular (articularis)*, *particular (particularis)*, *exemplary (exemplaris)*, *popular (popularis)*, *servile (famularis)*, which are illustrated as follows:

	An *articular* evil cruelly attacks the joints	(gout in hands,
Or thus:	An *articular* disease injures the joints	gout in foot).
Further:	A *particular* good aids the wretched.	
Or:	A vagrant tongue is harmful to its owner for this	
	Particular part is usually the injury of the whole body.	
Further:	The life of another is *exemplary* to me.	

(Whence Cato says: The life of another is a teacher for us.)

Further: *Popular* honor is gratifying to the hypocrite.
Further: A gentleman does not know how to endure *servile* obedience.

27. The Improper Use of Comparatives.
The following concerns comparatives in which words are arranged in many ways, such as *whiter (candidior)*, *more flowery (floridior)*, *poorer (pauperior)*, *richer (uberior)*, *wetter (humidior)*, *brighter (lucidior)*, *nearer (proximior)*, *more fallible (labilior)*, *more prosperous (prosperior)*, *weaker (languidior)*, *more skillful (callidior)*, *more fertile (fertilior)*, *more suitable (commodior)*, *freer (liberior)*, *more splendid (splendidior)*, *more useful (utilior)*, *more infirm (debilior)*, *more mobile (mobilior)*, *deeper (interior)*, *more lamentable (flebilior)*, *lower (inferior)*, *more outward (exterior)*, *farther in front of*

---

[25] *Am.* III. 4. 19.
[26] *Am.* I. 8. 43.

(anterior), farther beyond (ulterior), harsher (asperior), simpler (simplicior), better known (cognitior), shabbier (horridior), dirtier (sordidior), nobler (nobilior). And for these the following:

28.   A blush is challenged in a *whiter* face.
Further: Spring paints the ground in a *more flowery* garment.
Further: Unambitious oats increase with a *poorer* beard.
Further: The thief flees his pursuers with *fuller* stride.
Further: The moon moistens the earth with a *wetter* cycle.
Further: The day regains its breath with a *brighter* torch.
Further: I attend upon the king in a *nearer* place.
Further: The sun seeks it setting with a *more perishable*
                   movement.
Further: Fate gives new life to the defendant with a *more prosperous*
                   laugh.
Further: The good flourish with *weaker* success.
Further: The fox excells in *more cunning* slyness.
Further: A corn field sprouts from *more fertile* earth.
Further: The powerful revel in *more comfortable* living.
Further: Venus relies on a *freer* judgment.
Further: Leaders flourish with *more splendid* apparel.
Further: The wise excel by reason of *more useful* counsel.
Further: The poor lead with a *weaker* sound.
Further: Treacherous fate rejoices in a *swifter* flight.
Further: The mind of the wise works from a *deeper* home.
Further: The enemy announces wars with a *more tearful*
                   trumpet.
Further: Pluto restrains the wicked in the *lower* lake.
Further: Anger is revealed by the *more external* sign of the
                   countenance.
Further: The end lacks *earlier* success.
Further: A promise languishes with *further* delay.
Further: A bramble bush is fortified by a *rougher* tooth.
Further: A harlot shows favor with a *simpler* regard.
Further: Dogma shines by *better known* teaching.
Further: Old age is dirty because of *shabbier* neglect.
Further: Ruddy skin uses a *dirtier* deceit in its filthiness.
Further: The lion excells in *nobler* wrath.

(Whence in Lucan:

     The wrath of lions is noble.[27]

For it spares its conquered enemies.)

---

[27] *Phars.* VI. 487; in this section Matthew is illustrating the license which versification gives to proper Latin grammar, as he explains in the following paragraph.

29. An Explanation of the Construction of Improper Comparatives.

29. An Explanation of the Construction of Improper Comparatives. Further, lest it seem to someone starving and jejune of grammatical skill, that the construction in the preceding examples is improper and incorrect because they are not construed with the ablative without a preposition, or with a nominative, with *quam,* the adverb of comparison, the answer must be that comparatives occur in constructions in two ways: in combination and by itself. **30.** In combination, when there follows an ablative signifying one of the things compared or the nominative with the adverb *quam* interposed. Nor is "one of the things being compared" meaningless, because whenever any two things are compared in some circumstances, it is necessary that that circumstance be attributed to both of the two being compared; to one more strictly, and to the other less strictly. **31.** It is used absolutely when the thing being compared is reduced to its positive form with the adverb "very" added. This occurs in Statius when he speaks of Polynices:

He was loftier, with great stride and towering limbs.[28]

That is "very high." In Virgil:

Sadder she was, drowning her shining eyes with tears:[29]

that is "very sad." I say this comparison is used absolutely by reason of construction not in meaning: in construction, because a declinable does not follow that which signifies the thing to which the comparison is made; but not in meaning, because the addition is understood in the adverb "very." **32.** However, according to some the improper use of things being compared is three-fold: in meaning, in construction, and in function. But a treatment of these must be put off until another time. Likewise, in the preceding pentameters, comparatives are not used in combination but absolutely, that is, by being explained in parts. As in this example: "With poorer beard," that is "very poor." And similar examples should be similarly understood.

33. Moreover, there are many other adjectives whose beauty and grace can form a marriage in poetic measure, such as *succinct (succinctus), sophistic (sophisticus), prophetic (propheticus), prodigal (prodigus), vicarious (vicarius).* And of these the following are examples:

> *Succinct* brevity prepared in words and measure goes the
>   whole length,
>   And the lyrics lacking brevity are awry.

Further, concerning the secret hypocrite:[30]

> The *sophistic* soul and face are not in tune,
>   The pious exterior and the wolf within tear at each other.

---

[28] *Theb.* I. 414.
[29] *Ep.* I. 228.
[30] *De hypocrita cucullato:* "hooded hypocrite." It is likely Matthew is referring to his enemy Arnulf.

Further: Frauds are bared by the word and the countenance
            For *prophetic* guilt bears the markings of revealed crime.
Further: Red is mixed in with compatible brightness, the
                    pleasing
            Little lips give *prodigal* reminder of roses.
Further: Let the muse be without the sword and Pallas be
                    the *vicarious* sword,
            Because what is short in armor, let him supply with
                    richness of speech.

34. An Example of the Word "Preamble." Further, there follows an example concerning the word *preamble (preambulus),*[31] which echoes Epicurus. For he has the stomach of a spouse and protruding throat, "one born to consume food," his god is his stomach, his glory is amid confusion, his end is destruction, onto his stomach the testicles of Saturn have been cast, with the birth of lust every day the appetite for pleasure abounds more fully, which gathers delight from an inborn relish for adultery through foods that are teeming with spices; if his members respond to the lead of his belly they will grow to infinity. About him thus:

> His throat is wanton and the *protruding* mass of his belly
> Fortells the coming of its booming master.

35. Further, if in the introduction of examples the purpose of refreshing delicate ears frequently becomes a diversion to other related matter, yet it should not be attributed to an unsuitable digression, should it seem that I fall into that fault, about which Horace speaks;

> Works with serious beginnings and great promises
> Often have one or two purple patches so stitched on
> That they glitter far and wide.[32]

For as Tullius testifies,[33] similarity is the mother of sufficiency and variety banishes boredom. As a remedial endearment for boredom, we give strength to different factions, and charming things can be placed among the weighty, and pleasant things among serious things, thus, because they would in no way contradict its main purpose. Whence Horace says:

> It is not enough for poems to be beautiful, they
>   must have charm.[34]

---

[31] Literally "what walks before." The following lines reflect the medieval notion that the doctrine of Epicureanism centered on physical pleasure.

[32] *Ars Poet.* 14.

[33] Cic. *Inv.* I. 41. 76.

[34] *Ars Poet.* 99.

He also says in the same work:

> He has won every point who has blended profit with pleasure
> At once instructing and delighting the reader.[35]

36. Further, infinite are the substantives and also adjectives in which there is manifold ornamentation of words, and a graceful marriage can be detected. But because infinity is the step-mother of instruction and the friend of confusion (for infinities do not fall under any kind of calculation), after these premises, we should proceed to examples of the position of verbs. First of all, verbs of the first conjugation are to be dealt with; although they are limitless, it will be that much too artificial to present a limited doctrine or instruction about infinities. Moreover, no one here expects an exemplification except with regard to those verbs which get less exposure from common usage. **37.** And again, since in the above examples of many words the exemplary position has been exhausted, let a restrained brevity of examples suffice for the present. There are these: *I place the skull-cap upon (pilleo), I prosper (prospero), I impoverish (paupero), I perpetuate (perpetuo), I ennoble (purpuro), I make festive (festivo), I entitle (intitulo), I drop a syllable (syncopo), I sieze upon (confisco), I recreate (integro), I am jealous (zelotypo), I drop a letter (apocopo), I intoxicate (inebrio), I entice (inesco), I turn aside (exorbito), I beg (mendico), I decorate (phalero), I bury (intumulo), I intimate (intimo), I make friendly to myself* (amico), *I adore (adoro), I accuse (insimulo), I change (altero), I adopt (adopto), I entrap (illaqueo), I entangle (intrico), I introduce (importo), I defile (sordido), I sell formally (mancipo), I sicken (morbito), I emancipate (emancipo), I squander (dialpido),* There are also many others; but what is lacking in enumeration may it be supplied in examples.

About Verbs Which Give Color to Verses.

	Let the golden head-dress *be placed* on the distinguished locks.
Further:	Let the mystical head-dress *be placed* on the deserving head.
Or:	Varied fortunes *make prosperous* adverse conditions.
Further:	A lavish table *impoverishes* a lofty house.
Further:	A prosperous lot knows not how *to perpetuate* fidelity.
Further:	A bond pleasing to the lips *ennobles* the teeth.
Or:	Constant redness *ennobles* pleasing lips.
Further:	Golden vessels *make festive* humble food.
Further:	A noble author *entitles* a noxious work.
Further:	The erect organ *weakens* with sounds of copulation.
Further:	The king is used to *confiscating* the property of the people.
Further:	Being honored with favor *heals* damage to the affections.
Further:	Rufinus is jealous for a drought of power.

---

[35] *Ars. Poet.* 344.

38. There follows an example concerning this verb *he drops a syllable (apoco-pat)* concerning two rivals, one of whom was caught by the other in copula-tion, thus:

> Alas, the rival fearing his rival *cuts short a thrust,*
> And his erect organ, plowing, lacks the merited harvest.

Further, concerning Rufus, whose eyes an inflamation is destroying, thus:

> Intercourse with the harlot *inebriates* Rufinus,
> Or rather his filthy love *entices* the watery eyes of
> the prostitute.

Further: When love rules, virtue *turns aside.*
            Reason *goes begging,* law is inoperative.
Further: Hypocrites *embellish* their evil with a mask of piety.

(Whence in Juvenal: and after discoursing on virtue
            They wiggle their buttocks.)[36]

Further: Pallor *buries* the wealth of the rich mouth.
Further: Noxious anger *intimates* a fatal wrong.
Further: Taught to help himself *he makes a friend* of his work.

In Statius: But first Oenides *adores* the deity with his customary prayers.[37]

Further: The buffoon *accuses* the gentleman of a false crime.

(And in Ovid: O that I may be called rash
            To have accused a gentleman of false crimes.)[38]

Further: Faithless fate *changes* human conditions.
Further: The lover *accepts* the terms of the desired virgin.
Further: May Venus conquer and *entrap* unbriddled necks.
Further: An ornamented appearance pleases with its art:
                an anxious
            Lover at pains to please, *entwines* hair with hair.
Further: Sorrow *introduces* the significations of injury.
Further: A rude conversation *defiles* distinguished dignity.
Further: Gracious faithfulness *delivers* to what has been
                promised to a sacred observance.
Further: A plague *sickens* those heedless of the air.
Further: Wicked offspring *emancipates* judgment; When his
                Father is dead, he delights in squandering his
                father's wealth.
Further: The sacred victim *strikes* the harmless ox with a
                hammer.
Further: Wars *precede* the days of Caesar's justice.

(In Ovid: Valor *fell* early to the lot of the Caesars.)[39]

---

[36] *Sat.* II. 21.
[37] *Theb.* III. 470.
[38] *Her.* VI. 21.
[39] *Ars.* I. 184.

Further: The figures of the verse-maker *beautifies* his work.
Further: On the saucers the family Vendome *carry on a war.*
Further: The dishonorable mind *employs* the moves it has learned.
Further: Take care not *to give the first-fruits* of what you cannot
               do fully.
Or: The avid lover *pays the first fruits* of the realm of shame.
(That is, he tastes the first fruits of shame.)
Further: The teaching tongue *pours* learning by drops into
               ears.
Further: The dignity of the father *lends honor* to an
               iniquitous heir.
Further: Red fidelity *throbs* in a red color.
Further: Designing love *arrogates* the kingdoms of propriety.
Further: Refusing *to degenerate* he desires *to be like his father.*
Further: Rufinus fears *to match syllables* with me.[40]
Further: Rufinus *boasts* that Thais belongs to him.
Further: Venus *struggles* with reason opposing her.
Further: This actor pushing back *unites buttocks with buttocks,*
               Thais is assaulted and the cloisters sigh.
Further: Though propriety *delays* with its virginal mouth,
               Ruddy age *deflowers and depreciates* the rose.
Further: The loquacious tongue relates what should be kept
               quiet,
        It *blabs* what it wishes to conceal with the zeal of silence.
(In Horace:

Lest anyone *blabs* what has been said.[41]

Boethius in his book *Categorical Syllogisms:* "Very often an older treatment of philosophy *brings into the open* things suitable to tender ears.")

Further: Pernicious Venus *weakens* diligence.
        The spirit of envy *taints* every good.

(Whence in the *Bucolics:*

Some eye *bewitches* my gentle sheep.[42]

For envy is the hatred of another's good fortune.)

Further: The thief desires *to appropriate* another's property.
Further: An expressive face usually *lays open* secrets.

(Hence in Ovid:

O how difficult it is not *to betray* crime with your face.)[43]

---

[40] The following verses appear to be directed toward Matthew's enemy Arnulf (Rufinus).
[41] *Ep.* I. 5. 26.
[42] Virgil, *Ecl.* III. 104.
[43] *Met.* II. 447.

Further: A malign tongue *makes a frayed fringe* of outstanding glory.

Further, an example of this verb *abound (exuberat)* was appraised above in the description of Davus, thus the following:

> The disease of a sick chest
> *Spreads* into many persons.[44]

Further: The virgin *laughs loud* at the wicked work of the
                pander.

39. Further, there are many verbs in this and in other conjugations; because their position is ordinary and can be assigned easily and also has been assigned in the above examples, the listener may change their forms according to their similarity to the preceding examples with regard to the rest of the verbs, lest he tend to rely on the verses of others: for he swims away without an area of difficulty whose head is sustained by the support of someone else.

40. Further, in the previously given examples the procedure had to take up pentameters rather than hexameters so that the designation of elegy be noted, because this name holds sway in elegiac verses and in pentameters, and also because in the stated view it seemed good to instill the current patterns and examples in my own hearing. And again, because it is a lighter matter to inflict wounds than to heal them, to begin verses than to finish them. Likewise the pentameter ought to be the termination of the idea which is contained in the hexameter, the lighter part should have been presented to the listener in close contact so that it adapted the pentameters to its preceding hexameters as if by way of grafting.

41. Again, examples had to be given by supplying verses rather than clauses so that I might show the listener the whole advantage in verses rather than in incomplete clauses.

42. Moreover, there are certain braggarts and triflers, who have an urge to awkward presumption and presume to caw and abuse the meaning of words in this fashion: "He is redolent to injustice, savors of wickedness, has signed up for evil." To guard against and remedy this kind of deviation, the versifier must be practiced in the meaning of words so that he will not dare to join expressions which because of mutual incompatibility of meanings, and as it were craving separation, do not tolerate union in any marriage. For example, in "he is redolent of injustice" there exists a mutual incompatibility of meanings and no comprehension results. For "to be redolent" possesss a good meaning and "injustice" a bad meaning. And similar instances should be judged similarly; thus when one says "reddish fidelity" the contradiction occurs in what is added: for one word is destructive of the

---

[44] Part I. 53. v. 85.

meaning of the other, because the word "reddish" excludes "fidelity." Indeed, the color that luck gives wages wars; hence that common proverb: "When you see a trusted person who is red-headed, give glory to God." There is, though, contradiction in the adjunct when utterances are combined from which contradiction follows when they are taken singly.

43. Further, let verses lacking content and sweet-sounding trifles be excluded form this presentation, namely, frivolous collections of trifles, which like jesters or mimers play to ears with the sole appeal of consonance, which can imitate a lifeless cadaver, a storeroom without wine, a sheaf without grain, rations without seasoning. They can be compared to a distended bladder which has expanded with a noisy windiness and lacking beauty dribbling the sound, drawing its beauty from only the windiness of its own swelling: namely, the leonine verses whose beauty, like the very reason for their name, is unknown: among these, certain flute-players and those unskilled in the performance of the leonines are especially proud. **44.** But if harmony be excluded from the above small items of song, the verse, beggarly, as it were, and deprived of its salable garb, will be like the trunk of a figtree, useless wood. **45.** And yet not all verses of this kind are to be rejected, but only those in which, beggarly and without taste in ideas, fault is met with which is called dry and bloodless, hence in Horace:

> He crawls on the ground excessively safe and fearful
> of the storm.[45]

Therefore trifles of song must be emphasized more sparingly and elegiac verses more constantly. For in melodious sounds there is little or no elegance and, as it were,

> A rare bird in the world and much like a black swan.[46]

And again, whoever is skilled in elegiac verses is skilled also in songs, but not conversely.

46. There are some ragged expressions which being, as it were anathematized, and unworthy of the company of the rest, should be completely banished from metrical measure; Such as these: "Furthermore, however, also," and categorizations of this kind, that is, having common meanings, which because they detract from the beauty of the entire meter, ought to be completely eliminated from the meter. For there are few conjunctions and adverbs which should be placed in meter unless necessity demands it.

---

[45] *Ars. Poet.* 28.
[46] *Sat.* VI. 165.

[III. THE QUALITY OF EXPRESSION]

1. There is still to be treated the third point of the mentioned distinction, namely, quality or the manner of expression. For verse very often draws more of its beauty from the manner of expression than from the substance of what is said, as is clear in this example:

You my lord, you my husband, you my brother were.[1]

Neither ornateness of meaning, nor the surface charm of the words contributes elegance, but the way it is expressed. For there are three things contributing tone in versemaking: polished words, color of expression and inner charm. There are three figures in the above example; namely: zeugma at the end, because three clauses are united by the verb "were" placed in the final clause. Again in the same example there is a rhetorical color, namely repetition: for the pronoun "you" is repeated three times. Dialyton or asyndeton may also be found in this example since several separate clauses are presented singly and without a copulative conjunction. **2.** Indeed, as in material things the matter of a statue is rough and not outstanding in value until polished by an eager artist it becomes more pleasing, so in the meter of words the matter is rough and awkward until by skillful placing it is revealed as having some figure or trope or possessed of rhetorical color. And since figures, tropes and rhetorical colors are set forth in this third section, of the mentioned division, those things which concern prosodic ability or theory are to be explained, and figures are to be treated first.

3. The Nature and Number of Figures. "Schemas," as Isidore's *Etymologiae* testifies, are interpreted as "figures."[2] Although seventeen figures are rather frequently found, nevertheless, those which can be more elegantly fitted in the practice of versification are to be used, namely these: *zeugma, hypozeuxis, anaphora, epanalepsis, anadiplosis epizeuxis, paronomasia, parhomoeon, schesisonomaton, homoeoteleuton, polyptoton, polysyndeton, dialyton* or *asyndeton.*[3] **4.** Since we have towards the beginning treated the figures of *hypozeuxis* and *zeugma*, we must next see what *anaphora* is.

---

[1] Ovid. *Her.* III. 52.

[2] Isadore of Seville's great work of twenty books illustrates the encyclopedic tendency of the age and made him a primary promotor of the seven liberal arts. He was much read as the great source of classical thought.

[3] It is to be noted that the figures here listed are for the most part repetition variations, some of them particular to the Latin language.

5. *Anaphora*[4] is duplicate positioning at the beginning of two sequent verses, as in Juvenal concerning Pontia:

> You killed two, did you, you savage viper?
> You killed two?[5]

And following is a more familiar example of Rufus and his concubine Rufa:

> Rufus, Rufa prefers the smell of money to you;
>   Rufus, the virile members of the public are taking your
>   place.

6. *Epanalepsis*[6] is the duplication at the end of a verse of a word placed at its beginning. As in Juvenal:

> Grows then the love of money as money itself grows.[7]

7. *Anadiplosis*[8] is the repetition at the beginning of the following verse of the word which terminates the first verse, as in the *Bucolics:*

> Let Tityrus be Orpheus,
> Orpheus in the woods, Arion among the dolphins.[9]

My own example concerning these three figures goes like this:

> Love knows not how to determine value, to be sparing it
>   knows not;
>   Love knows not how to disperse unequal inheritance.

Note the anaphora in this example because the word "knows not" is repeated at the beginning of each verse; there is also epanalepsis because the same word, namely "knows not" is placed at the beginnig of the verse and is repeated at the end of the verse; And the example also includes anadiplosis for the expression placed at the end of the verse is repeated at the beginning of the next.

8. *Epizeuxis*[10] is the immediate repetition of the same word in the same verse for a greater expression of feeling, as in Virgil:

> O thus, O thus, it is my will to go into the darkness.[11]

---

[4] Also called *repetitio.*

[5] *Sat.* VI. 641.

[6] *Complexio.*

[7] *Sat.* XIV. 139.

[8] *Gradatio.*

[9] VIII. 55; Arion, a horse endowed with speech and the gift of prophecy sent to Adrastus by Neptune.

[10] *Conduplicatio.*

[11] *Aen.* IV. 660.

Or thus about the pretended flight of a girl friend so that the lover might be tortured more fully:

> Flora flees: flees that she may return; her mind's intention
> Is concealed from her forehead; fleeing in body she
> returns in intention.

9. *Paronomasia*[12] is the use of cognate terms which agree in their beginning or ending. Now this figure is formed in two ways. It is formed usually through the agreement of initial letters or syllables, as in the following manner:

> Fame fosters meager merit in a lunatic but
> not in a lover;
> It is befitting to depreciate the price of evil.

Or thus concerning the luxury-loving monks whose blackened wickedness is hidden under a garment of false religion:[13] They incarcerate many kinds of viands in the work-house of the belly and belch forth ornate thanks to the Most High. About them someone said this:

> It is not glory they know how to belch forth, but garlic;
> They gather more in salmon than from Solomon.

Paronomasia occurs also in the compatibility of final syllables as shown in the following example: After comparing the king to the pope, or the thief to the cenobite monk, thus, that is, that approval be ascribed to pope or monk, blame be imputed to the king or thief: in this manner:

> The latter sees, the former seizes; one edifies, the other
> vilifies;
> This one is acrid that one sacred; one elevates, the other
> denigrates.

10. What is called *paranomeon* comes next.[14] Paranomeon is the repeated use of the same letter or syllable at the beginning of three words juxtaposed. However, this figure varies in three ways. For it occurs very often at the beginning of a verse, very often in the middle, and very often at the end. At the beginning of a verse, as in Vergil's *Aeneid:*

> Impius fury within
> Sitting supreme on savage arms.[15]

---

[12] *Adnominatio.*
[13] Matthew once again attacks Arnulf.
[14] Alliteration.
[15] I. 294.

These three words, namely "sitting, supreme, savage" placed in juxtaposition at the beginning of the verse begin with the semivocalic "s." — It occurs again in the middle of a verse, as in the same author:

> Who far and wide swarm the lapping liquid lakes,
>   the thorn and thicket.[16]

Insofar as those three expressions "laping, liquid, lakes," juxtaposed in the middle of the verse begin with the same letter, namely "l," this forementioned figure can be identified. For the middle is whatever is contained between the two extremes. It also occurs at the end, as in the same author:

> To me alone Cassandra sang such sorrows.

The following is my own example of two impatient rivals of a shared[17] concubine:

> Deep desire distresses the foolish with longing to ravish,
>   The mind of the lover laments love, rejects an equal
>   sharing similar sighs.

Whence in Ovid:

> In fellowship neither love nor thrones stand sure.[18]

Or thus about the beggar-woman seeking alms from the king for her infirm husband:

> Royal ruler, redress with gentleness conditions of misery; my
>   master is ill:
> Give, giving gifts is and will be honorable, contribute
>   resources.

11. *Schesisonomaton* occurs when a number of distinct words are joined by a certain similarity, as in Statius:

> Horseman Iphis, foot-soldier Argus, charioteer Abas lie
>   wounded.[19]

Or this concerning the inconstancy of Fortune:

> Love of fate is odius, law is treacherous, laughter has its
>   tears, permanence is inconstant, and faith is false.

12. *Homoeoteleuton* [20] is the exactly similar ending of a number of words, as in Horace:

> Repair, beware, take care that you do not stumble and
>   smash your valued charge.[21]

---

[16] IV. 526; Matthew's version is really untranslatable. See Faral p. 170, n. a.
[17] III. 183.
[18] *Ars.* III. 564.
[19] *Theb.* VIII. 448.
[20] *Similiter desinens.*
[21] *Ep.* I. 13. 19.

Or thus:

> Choosing, bending, seeking, strengthening, soothing,
> > preserving
> Vows, pact in defilement by gifts, faith by love.

In the hexameter verse the example pertains because of verbs of similar endings; in the second verse, the pentameter, the figure polyptoton is exemplified.

13. *Polyptoton* [22] occurs when the cases in a group are distinguished by the variety in endings as is shown in the above example.

14. *Polysyndeton* is the copulative connection of clauses along with many conjunctions, as in Virgil:

> Acamas and Thoas, and Neoptolemus, the son of Peleus.[23]

Or thus:

> Ruffus, you harm with both javelin and deceit;
> > Ruffa reveals a complexion marked with the forecast of
> > fraud.

15. *Dialyton* (or *asyndeton*) [24] is the contrary of the preceding figure, namely, the distinctness of a number of clauses left unjoined by any union by conjunctions, as in Virgil:

> Bring firebrands quickly, unfurl sails, lean on the oars.[25]

Or this:

> The plague of love is very welcome, a very delightful poison,
> > A pleasing punishment, a fragrant passion, a delightful
> > evil;

Or this:

> Love is an unjust judge, it cannot discern primacy,
> > It binds all with a similar shackle.

A distinction should be made between dialyton and schesisonomaton, although a separation of clauses may occur in both figures. For the difference is this: schesisonomaton consists of nouns in which a verb is never or rarely interposed, nor does it completely reject conjunctions; dialyton does indeed admit verbs, but in such a way that conjunctions are excluded from its clauses.

---

[22] A variation of *traductio* which is the repetition of a word in a different form, voice or case; *Vota, datis, stuprum, foedus, amore, fidem.*

[23] *Aen.* II. 263.

[24] Or *dissolutio.*

[25] *Aen.* IV. 594.

16. Moreover, we must note that what Isidore states concerning this figure paranomeon is not to be passed over.[26] He says: "But if the number three be exceeded it will not be the figure, but the contrary of the figure." He himself then presents the example in which Ennius uses this figure, saying:

> Thou O Titus, Tatus, tyrant, taught thou all this to thyself.[27]

17. In the foregoing examples may the sensitive listener seek nothing except that the example and the exemplar correspond to and satisfy the intention of the exemplifier. For long ago I sought a truce with a detractor so that no verse be held as assertive, but be considered as included by way of example.[28]

18. The Kinds and Number of Tropes.

The following concerns tropes. The Greek "trope" is translated into Latin as "a manner of speaking." Tropes occur for the charm of speech and without beauty of meaning. Although they number thirteen, still those points must be recalled which ought to be deeply impressed on the versifier. The first to be treated is metaphor.

19. A *metaphor*[29] is the transferred use of some word. Now, this trope has four divisions. This most often takes place in transference from the animate to the animate, from the inanimate to the inanimate; from the animate to the inanimate and from the inanimate to the animate.

20. A metaphor can go from the animate to the animate, as in Virgil:

> He mounted the winged horses[30]

The epithet is that for birds, namely from the bearing of wings; but it is attributed metaphorically to the horse; both of these are animate.
Or thus:

> Rufus, lacking in reason, caws like a crow; for practice of
> Deceit he expends the work of his mind and his voice.

Here similarly, what is proper to crows, namely to caw, is attributed to Rufus. —**21.** Secondly, a metaphor may be formed in going from the

---

[26] Matthew's inclusion of this detail which more properly belongs above where he introduces the figure suggests he happened to find it in Isadore which he had before him.

[27] *Annales*, 113.

[28] Here Matthew seems to protest too much, saying the verses referring to Rufinus are examples, not intentional invective.

[29] *Translatio.*

[30] As Faral notes p. 72, Matthew attributes this quotation erroneously; Isidore's *Etymologiae*, I. 36. 3.

inanimate to the inanimate object when what belongs to one inanimate thing is assigned to another inanimate object by some transference of meaning. As in Virgil:

> All aglow is the work and the fragrant honey is redolent
>   with thyme.[31]

This characteristic of a flower, namely, to be redolent, is attributed to honey: both of these are inanimate. Similarly, the following can be the example of a person priding himself on beauty's flower:

> The distinction of voice clashes with an obstacle to
>   his arrogance, his appearance. . .

Or thus:

> Though Flora shines with a very rich appearance of
>   character,
>   The iciness of her mind grows green, crime has its taste
>   in her mouth.

In this example the same thing as above can be identified. For what is proper of flowers, namely to grow green, is attributed to iciness; both of these are inanimate. —**22.** The metaphor can be made in a third way: going from the inanimate to the animate, as in Statius concerning Adrastus:

> He lacked issue of the stronger sex, but was fruitful
> In female offspring.[32]

And again in Ovid concerning Galatea:

> More flowery than a snowy meadow, etc.[33]

In these examples what pertains to inanimate things, namely to flower, to be come fruitful, is applied by transference to animate things, namely, Adrastus and Galatea. Or thus:

> A modest virgin is in flower with her maidenhead intact,
>   The flower betrays to all the given charms of her speech.

In this there is a metaphor, because what is proper to an inanimate thing, namely to be in flower, is applied to a maiden. —**23.** The metaphor can be made in a fourth way, going from the animate to the inanimate, as in Statius:

> And the field died at the hissing.[34]

And again in Ovid:

> The waves of ocean know not what master to obey.[35]

---

[31] *Georgics,* IV. 169.
[32] *Theb.* I. 393.
[33] *Met.* XIII. 790. Though Matthew wrenches the text somewhat, the illustration holds.
[34] *Theb.* V. 528.
[35] *Tristia,* I. 2. 26.

The metaphor consists in the fact that to die and not to know, which belong to animate things, are attributed to the field and the waves. Or this concerning shipwreck:

> The lightning roars, and the sea's madness thunders,
>> The waves are haughty, and daring night is born at
>>> midday.

—24. Here the four-fold metaphor can be identified. Yet some metaphors are antistrophes, that is, reversible and some are not. Reversible, as in Virgil: "the rowing of the wings." This can be reversed so that it reads, "the wings of the oars." Some cannot be reversed, as the above "and the field died at the hissing:" there is no reverse here. Indeed this trope by a certain special prerogative has a singular pre-eminence among the other tropes and should be used often especially by verse-makers: for it adapts a special beauty to the metrical arrangement.

25. Antithetum. [36] Furthermore, the following deals with *antithetum*. Antithetum is contraposition, when contraries are opposed to contraries, as in Ovid:

> The cold fights with the heat, the humid with the dry,
>> The soft with the hard, the weightless with the heavy. [37]

Or thus concerning the prodigal person reproving the greedy:

> I feast, you fast; I give, you seek; I rejoice, you are sad;
>> I drink, you thirst; you retain, I pay out, I hope, you fear.

This trope occurs in four ways: through constructions, through adjectivals, through substantives, and through verbs. **—26.** Through construction as in Ovid:

> She killed her father, I rescued Thoas from death;
>> She deserted her fatherland; my Lemnos has me still. [38]

—27. Through adjectives, as in the same author:

> The cold fights with the hot, etc. [39]

—28. Through substantives, as in the book of *Cosmography* of Bernard:

> Poverty in the stars of Codrus, riches of Croesus,
>> The incest of Paris, and the shame of Hippolytus. [40]

---

[36] *Contentio* or *Antithesis*.
[37] *Met*. I. 19.
[38] *Her*. VI. 135.
[39] *Met*. I. 19.
[40] I. 41.

—29. Through verbs, as in these verbs "I eat, you fast," and similar ones. Or thus concerning the soldier reproving the cleric:

> I dare, you dread: I put to flight, you yield;
>   I fight, you are idle; I get up, you lie down; I am
>   virgorus, you are failing; I press on, you lurk.

Observe, no part of the above verses lacks its antithesis: for each of the expressions works to form an anthithesis.

30. Metonymy.[41] Again, *metonymy* is a change which occurs in three ways: when the thing found is accepted for the finder or conversely; when the container is accepted for the thing contained or conversely; or when the possession is accepted for the possessor or conversely. But because the first two modes are used less often by writers, the third way will be pursued, namely, when the container is used for the thing contained or conversely. **31.** For this trope is reversible or convertible. The container is used for the contents, as in Statius speaking of Tydeus:

> Look at this field
> Everywhere steaming from my sword.[42]

that is "the corpses contained in the field." And likewise concerning the gods who are deprived of the benefit of hospitality on earth:

> The gods are deprived of the honor of hospitality, the
> Sky might have blushed for the rejection by the world.

32. Contents are used for the container, as in Statius:

> But after fury and valor generous with life
> Had sent forth their spirits.[43]

"Valor" is presented for "the valorous" in whom it is contained. Similarly in Lucan:

> No loyalty ever chose the wretched for friends.[44]

that is, "no loyal person." Likewise in the topography set forth earlier:[45]

> The oak tree, nourisher of swine, salutes the sky with its
> Neck and regards its Jove with prayerful speech.

that is, "heaven in which is contained its Jupiter, to whom the oak is consecrated."

---

[41] Also *Denominatio;* a variation of this is *metalepsis* or *transumptio.*

[42] *Theb.* II. 702.

[43] *Theb.* VIII. 406.

[44] *Phars.* VIII. 535.

[45] This refers to *Description of Place,* Part I, 111.

33. Synecdoche.[46] Further, *synecdoche* is the substitution of a part for the whole or conversely, as in Horace when speaking to his book through prosopopeia: [47]

> If it happens that someone inquires my age, let him know
> I have completed eleven Decembers four times.[48]

that is, "years." Similarly:

> The woman born to injure longs for crime,
>   Powerful in deceit, the initial seed of evil.

34. The part is used for the whole. For what is said generally is given here to be understood particularly. Whence in Ovid:

> Refrain from pouring out on all the crime of a few.[49]

—35. Synecdoche occurs in a second way, as in Vergil's *Bucolics:*

> Now the year is at the fairest; [50]

that is, "part of the year," that is, "spring." the following is an example about the concubine of Rufus:

> The child of Rufis is ruddy, indeed the instrument
>   Proclaims the potter, the father sins in the face of his child.

In this example the whole is said to become ruddy because of the face.

36. What *Periphrasis* [51] is will be stated in what follows, where the change of material is discussed.

37. The Three-Fold Mode of Epithetum. We have already explained what *epithetum* is.[52] It occurs in three ways: through constructions, through adjectives, and through verbs. **—38.** Through constructions as in Statius:

> The alders that love the sea bend to the ground, the
>   Elms that give friendly shelter to the vines.[53]

---

[46] *Intellectio.*

[47] Or *conformatio:* personification.

[48] *Ep.* I. 20, 26.

[49] *Ars.* III. 9.

[50] III. 57.

[51] *Circuito:* stating the same idea in various ways. Matthew does not discuss this figure as he states.

[52] See Part I. 64, "On Epithets" and the following discussion of description.

[53] *Theb.* VI. 106.

—**39.** Through verbs, as in my own example of familiar topography: [54]

> The flowers give fragrance, the grass grows, the trees bear,
> > Fruit overflows, the birds chatter, the river murmurs, the
> > > air is cool.

—**40.** Again through construction; so, in the same topography:

> The charming murmur of water, the harmonious voice of
> > birds, etc.

—**41.** Through adjectives, as in the book of *Cosmography* of Bernard:

> The red turtledove, the savory salmon, the very fat shad,
> > Short gardo, long barbel, large sole. [55]

42. Metalepsis or Climax. [56] Metalepsis, or climax, is the gradual progression of clauses so that the final word of a prior clause is the beginning of the next, as in Virgil's *Bucolics:*

> The savage lioness follows the wolf, the wolf himself the she-goat.
> The wanton goat follows the flowering clover. [57]

In this example, the ending of the first clause is the beginning of the subsequent clause as to construction, not as to meter. But what is lacking in meter is supplied in construction. The following example is clearer:

> Anger stirs up strife, strife battles, battles death,
> > Death tears, tears move the gods, the gods grant
> > > assistancm.

43. Allegory. Further, allegory is a way of speaking in which the understanding differs from the meaning of the words, as in the *Bucolics:*

> I sent ten golden apples, tomorrow I will send a second ten. [58]

Here, according to Isidore, by "ten golden apples" the ten Eclogues of the *Bucolics* are understood. Or the following concerning a handsome but arrogant person:

> Loudly a nut complains of its kernel; the depth of winter
> > does not
> Know what the vernal surface proclaims to the lands.

---

[54] Part I. 111.

[55] I. 437.

[56] Cf. *anadiplosis* or *gradatio.*

[57] II. 63.

[58] III. 70.

By "nut" the blooming exterior, by "kernel" the depth of winter, are presented for your understanding. Again, my own example in the verses about Afra and Milo, so that the work might by an example give testimony to the author.

> The vine lacks fruit, and owing its bare branches to the
> Weather, with poorer foliage crawls along the ground.

By "the vine lacking fruit" one is given to understand the contempt of Milo for the barren Afra. — Although there are seven types of this trope, we will discuss one of lesser treatment, namely, the aenigma.

44. Aenigma. *Aenigma* is the obscurity of meaning hidden by a certain cover of words, as in Virgil:

> Tell me in what lands (and you shall be my great Apollo)
> Heaven's space is not more than three ells broad.[59]

Or this:

> My mother brought me forth, she also is brought forth
> from me:

This example is understood to refer to becoming solid. Similarly concerning Narcissus:

> A lover seeks what he has, what he loves, what he seeks.
> It is characteristic of a lover that though he abounds in his
> personal possessions, he is destitute.

And this seems impossible unless it be understood of the love of Narcissus.

45. Figures and tropes have been presented, things which seemed more necessary to this little work; consequently rhetorical colors would have to be treated had they not already been clarified by another. Hence, lest I seem to repair the present work with another's patches, they will be omitted since my own treasury is sufficient for me. Besides, when we spoke of figures and tropes, rhetorical colors are not exlcuded. For certain figures and certain tropes seem to correspond to certain rhetorical colors, of which we should make a collation. They are the following, which in combination seem to have a harmony in association: *antithetum* and *contentio, anaphora* and *duplicatio, paronomasia* and *annominatio, epanalepsis* and *repetitio, schesisonomaton* and *membrum orationis* or *articulus, dialyton* and *dissolutum, polysyndeton* and *conjunctum, metalepsis* or *climax* and *gradatio,* of which an example ought to be repeated:

> Talk summons praise, praise rewards, rewards stirs up the
> mind,
> The mind zeal, zeal song, song stimulates the work.

---

[59] *Buc.* III. 105.

46. Indeed, the tenth repeated mention of verses of this kind will give pleasure. For whoever in verses of this kind, with only one word-figure placed in the first clause, and the following expressions joined by similar form, labors to the tenth phrase, that versifier will seem to me to be adept rather because of the difficulty than of elegance. Therefore, because it just happens to anyone at all to go to Corinth, let the hissing Rufinus try his strength here — he was accustomed to be Teiresias in elegiacs, even Polyphemus in the trifles of song. Taste is the judge of elegance and experience the arbitrator of difficulty or of truth.

47. Moreover, that the listener may know what remains to be investigated, let the assigned names of the rhetorical colors suffice for the present; these are: *repetitio, conversio, complexio, traductio, contentio, exclamatio, ratiocinatio, sententia, contrarium, membrum orationis* or *articulus, similiter cadens, similiter disinens, commixtio, annominatio, subjectio, gradatio, diffinitio, transitio, correctio, occupatio, disjunctio, conjunctum, adjunctum, conduplicatio, commutatio, dubitatio, dissolutio, praecisio, conclusio.*

48. Further, in the mentioned review it seemed to me that Elegy impressed images in my heart to recall the three parts of the foregoing division. But although

> There is not a lesser virtue than to seek to look upon one's
>   productions.
> I sang these things and it delights me to have sung them.

For:

> Wisdom is pleasing coin, once given it multiplies and grows;
> It knows not how to grow if it be kept silent.

49. It should be noted that the mentioned division is not created by opposites. For just as virtue does not exclude virtue, nor the rose the lily, nor the sapphire the pearl, but the things that singly are not useful but please when multiplied; similarly in meter one color does not exclude another nor one figure another; on the contrary, colors are more pleasing when accumulated and they add to each other's beauty with related benefits and greet one another with sisterly flattery; and even the three elements of the mentioned division can be given place in the same verse, as in Statius:

> A short reign is unsparing to the people.[60]

Here, concerning the first element, there is the ornament of interior meaning, for it is a general notion. As to the second element, the words are sufficiently formal. As to the third element, there is ornament in the quality of the expression, for here there is a certain kind of metaphor since what belongs to an animate being, namely to spare, is attributed metaphorically to an inanimate thing, namely a reign. Or there can be metonymy here, because the possession stands for the possessor, that is, the reign for the ruler.

---

[60] *Theb.* II. 446.

50. And if one be allowed to compare material things to words, just as in animate beings, as in man, we can consider three things, namely, the vital spirit, the beauty of the corporeal matter, and the upright manner of living; nor yet is the one exclusive of the other, but rather when joined they compare better and possess a more pleasing effect; so likewise in meter the charm of the inner meaning and the external ornament of words and the quality of the expression take to one another hospitably, and infrequently or rarely does one of them get a place by itself in a meter without the company of the other.

51. Further, to keep the course of the present introductory matter from wavering toward the fault of superfluity, since virtue is the mean effected between two vices, as Horace testifies,[61] and because you will go most safely in the middle,[62] so that a satisfactory presentation be made of the three elements of the foregoing division, we discussed above the first element, namely, the judging of ideas in things attributed to activity and person. In examples of adjectives, there is clear explanation also of different endings of verbs, or verbal ornamentation. A discussion of the third division, namely the quality of expression, is examined in the figures and tropes. **52.** But if perchance a bungler should venture to caw like a crow, saying that the same numbering came to him in the mentioned division, because the ornamentation of verses is treated in the first, second and third parts, the answer would be that in the first, second and third parts the ornamentation of verse is in fact treated but in three ways. For though the reason for treating them is unified, variety is valued in the manner of their treatment. First, because the ornament of inner meaning is discussed; second, the ornament of words; and third, the quality of expression. Hence, some rationale of order can be assigned to these three division. For just as in the mentioned divisions, meanings precede, words follow, and the quality of expression is subordinated to the third place, similarly in the performance of poetic ability imagination precedes the senses, speech follows as the interpreter of thought and then comes arrangement in the quality of expression. Prior to the idea is its conception, second is the invention of the words, and there is appended, naturally, the character of the subject matter or the arrangement of the treatment.

---

[61] Cf. *Ep.* I. 18. 9.
[62] Cf. Ovid. *Met.* II. 137.

[IV. THE TREATMENT OF MATERIAL]

1. The Treatment of Material. What follows is the treatment of the material in which certain poorly instructed students are accustomed to be crackbrained and stray shamefully from the path of proper doctrine; in school exercises they paraphrase the poetical fables and work out an expression after each word as if they intended a metrical commentary on the authors. But since undisciplined transgression should gain forgiveness, and perhaps when they are being misled by misleading teachers, their good interests should be looked to so that in the treatment of material they may try to imitate the customary outcomes, namely, so they may speak the truth or the probable. Nor should anyone attempt to render word for word as a steadfast translator.[1] **2.** For there are some words which, as if condemned, ought to be passed by in the course of the treatment; for if they are used, the entire part of the work is blackened rather than be drawing from it any ray of beauty; and this is on the authority of Homer. Hence Horace says of Homer:

> And when he has no hope that what he treats can gain
> glitter, he abandons it.[2]

For things understated should be filled in, the inharmonious should be enhanced, and the superfluous completely discarded.

3. Moreover, the material which anyone proposes to treat will be either untouched or treated previously by some poet. If it has been treated, you will have to proceed according to the trend of the poetic narration, with such regard that certain diffusions be not introduced which are affinitive but not pertinent to the principal theme, such as comparisons, poetic abuses, figurative constructions, arrangement of quantities and syllables. —**4.** This, not because the introduction of comparisons should be completely omitted, but they should be used more sparingly by contemporary

---

[1] Cf. Horace, *Ars. Poet.* 133.

[2] *Ars. Poet.* 150.

writers. They can be introduced because without them the figure goes off track and there will be no need of them here. **5.** Indeed, it was necessary for ancient authors to extend material with certain digressions and collateral ideas so that the paucity of material be profuse with poetic fancyings and bloom with artistic growth. This however is not permitted to contemporary versifiers. For the old has yielded to the incoming new. **—6.** Further, we ought not imitate abuses in the lengths of syllables. For truth or analogy need not be expressly demanded of those who had desire instead of reason. Indeed, what would be considered a fault for us, contributed to indulgence for them. Indeed, no transgression in the lengths of syllables is allowed in present times, except in two instances, namely, penthemimeris and synalepha. The penthemimeris, that is, five half-feet, is permitted to the novice, synalepha to all the advanced. **—7** Also figurative constructions should be eliminated from contemporary practice although they are introduced by the authors, as in Virgil's *Aeneid:*

And some mounted on tall steeds rampage in clouds of dust.[3]

Again in Statius:

This troop, three thousand in all, followed Adrastus.[4]

Here the figure is twofold in consequence of gender and number. **8.** Improper positions of words should also be avoided, as in Virgil's *Bucolics:* "He burned for Alexis."[5] And likewise in Statius: "As though breathless he panted after Phlegra's fight."[6] There are infinite abuses of this kind which are to be observed only, not extended. However, in this case, it behooves the moderns to excuse the ancients rather than imitate them. Indeed

The child still feels what the parents have perpetrated.

9. So, since in human speech three things occur or are imminent: art, fault, and figure; art we should imitate, fault we should banish completely, and figure demands support.

10. The Avoidance of the Ineffective Use of Words and Sentences.

Further, an ineffective use of words and sentences is to be guarded against: of words, as "they went where they could; and where they could not, they did not go."[6] This fault is perissologia, namely, a useless addition of too many words; pleonasm is the useless addition of a

---

³ *Aen.* VII. 625; *Pars arduus altis Pulverulentus equis furit. Pars* should agree with *arduus* and *Pulverulentus* in gender and number.

⁴ *Theb.* IV. 63; *Haec manus Adrastum numero ter mille secuti. Manus* and *secuti* do not agree in gender and number.

⁵ *Ecl.* II. 1.

⁶ Cf. *Conatus, Ars Grammatica,* III.

single word, as in Virgil: "Thus with her lips she spoke,"[7] and in Lucan: "thus he, Jupiter," Clearly "he" is superfluous. Tautology is the useless repetition of a word, although the repetition of a word is very often appropriate to the meaning and not useless. On the other hand, superfluity in sentences is called macrology, that is, a long speech covering matters that are not necessary. **11.** And it should be pointed out that suitable repetition is formed in three ways: for the purpose of an addition, for the purpose of clarification, and for the purpose of greater expressiveness. It occurs for the purpose of addition as in expository words and vivid sentences; in both instances an expression is repeated so as to add something, as in Statius:

> Most fair Astyr,
> Astyr, trusting his steed.[8]

A sentence is repeated in order to explain it, as in Lucan about Pompey and Caesar:

> Italy's fields are ablaze with savage destruction.[9]

And later he repeats the sentence so he might identify the savage destroyers, saying:

> The fury of Gaul is pouring over the frosty Alps.[10]

—And again a word is repeated for the purpose of expressiveness, as in Statius:

> Tydeus, to arms, to arms, ye men![11]

—Again, the sentence is repeated for vividness as in the refrain of the *Bucolics:*

> Bring him home from the city, my songs, bring Daphnis
> home.[12]

12. There are also many other faults which should be eliminated from the handling of matter, namely, acirologia, which is the improper use of a word, as in Statius concerning Tydeus:

> Nor did he have strength to hope for death.[13]

that is, "to fear," for hope pertains to good, fear, to evil.

—And amphibologia, which is ambiguity of construction, as

> Having crossed Halys, he will destroy many kingdoms.[14]

---

[7] *Aen* I. 614.
[8] The passage is from Virgil, *Aen.* X. 180.
[9] *Phars.* II. 534.
[10] *Phars.* II. 535.
[11] *Theb.* III. 348.
[12] *Ecl.* VIII. 84.
[13] *Theb.* II. 607.
[14] *Cresus perdet Alim transgressus plurima regna.*

—There are also other faults, like cacemphaton, or indistinct pronunciation, as:

Raise up your ears, Pamphyle.[15]

There are also many others, namely, eclipsis, tapinosis, cacosyntheton, and many more. Anyone who would wish to be familiar with descriptions of these should consult the *Barbarismus*.[16] Indeed, the instance of the above-mentioned faults should be ascribed to poet's license, not to their ignorance. For poets do not employ figures ignorantly but spontaneously and for the purpose of variety which takes away boredom.

13. How Things Not Fully Expressed Should be Expanded.
Up to this point we have said how superfluity should be pruned. The following shows how things said too sparingly should be expanded. For example, there is a certain order of succession in human actions. For certain actions precede others and some follow others. For example, in the specific practice of love a look comes first, then desire, approach, conversation, dalliance, and finally the anxious union of the two. For Ovid testifies:

What two have willed does not lack completion.[17]

Ovid testifies to those stages of action saying:

They come by their own measured steps.[18]

Similarly in the handling of material we should imitate the degrees of the actions in clear steps so there may be no break in the narrative just as there is none in the above-mentioned actions. Indeed Ovid seems to cut into or excise a middle portion of actions when he speaks of Inachus, saying:

Jupiter had seen Io coming from her father's stream,
And said, "O maiden worthy of Jove, and likely to make
Someone happy with your bed, etc."[19]

The coherence of this narrative is broken, for two steps are left out, namely desire and approach. Seeing and conversation, though, are joined as if they followed in natural sequence. But, as Ovid states at the end of his work:

I would have been ready to emend had it been permitted.[20]

---

[15] Terrence, *Andria*, V, 4. 30.

[16] Book III of the *Ars Grammatica* of Donatus; *eclipsis:* an omission, *tapinosis:* a depreciation, *cocosyntheton:* an incorrect connection of words.

[17] *Am.* II. 3. 16.

[18] *Ars.* I. 482.

[19] *Met.* I. 588-90.

[20] *Tristia,* I. 7. 40.

14. How Awkwardness Can be Changed for the Better.

The following shows how awkwardness in material previously treated can be changed for the better. For example, if in the treatment of material dealt with some rough spot has developed wherein the material becomes rather confused, muddled, and not ordered with sufficient artistry, as in Ovid, concerning the slaying of Argus, where he says:

> The recounting of words remained,[21]

and the rest which is inserted up to:

> He about to relate such things, . . .[22]

lest similar confusion occur, the material should be varied with the retention of equal weight in the meaning but the way of saying it improved, so that what is said by the poet with some involvement of confusion may be made clear by the exposition of narrative of equal value. **15.** Thus contemporaries will have to follow tenaciously, along two lines: the meaning of the material treated, the changing of words and varied joining of expressions; so that it cannot be attributed to poverty in judgment if someone wishes to appropriate the author's words and the same joinings.

16. Untouched Material.

So much concerning material previously used, namely, the poetic stories which the naked Garamantes[23] cultivate in the school exercises in verse writing. Next comes material not previously used; in its treatment one must especially look into practice so that the character of daily actions be similarly expressed with the help of words, to bring it about that the firm treatment of the matter seems to give material form to the object, namely, that what is heard correspond to the usage. **17.** Indeed, it will be a matter either of the attributes of a person or the attributes of the action. **18.** If it deals with the attributes of a person, the description ought to portray such a person as is preconceived by the essence of an imaginary description or conjecture, so that what earlier stood in one's thought may later be brought forth with the assistance of expression. For example, a girl

> Choose, to whom you will say, "You alone please me." [24]

what she was in pleasing you, let her be painted as such in your treatment, this to the extent of gaining acceptance. Likewise for bringing about blame, let her be represented so deformed as to be especially abhorrent to your sight and that of the public. **19.** If the attributes of an action are the concern, one will have to use conjecture and proceed according to the common

---

[21] *Meta.* I. 700.

[22] *Meta.* I. 713.

[23] In ancient history, a nomadic people dwelling in the Sahara.

[24] *Ars.* I. 41.

thinking of all and the authority of usage. In the attributes of the action, however, more than in the attributes of a person, a restrained brevity is to be used, so that the material be laid out clause by clause, unless there is involved a beauty of meaning as in the originals with metaphors, epithets, and the like. Indeed, because on the testimony of Boethius, contraries accompany contraries, just as things which displease when treated should be omitted, so likewise the beauty of meaning should be explained at greater length.

20. The Alteration of Material. Many things remain to be said regarding the treatment of material: but because our course yearns for its end, lest boredom spring up, let us have the following about the alteration of material; it indeed pertains to treatment. Alteration of material can be made in two ways: one is by altering the words and the sentences, but keeping equivalent meaning; the other is to alter the words but not the sentences.

21. The alteration of words and sentences is often made through periphrasis. Periphrasis is circumlocution. This trope takes place in two ways: either when the truth is splendidly set forth or when the foulness of the meaning is avoided through a circuitousness. The truth is splendidly set forth, as here is Virgil:

> Then indeed, Aurora, leaving the saffron bed of Tithonus,
> Was already showering the world with her first rays; [25]

so that the sense is "already it was becoming day." The following is an example of my own:

> Learning is the companion of usage; learning in school
>   Dies if interrupted, if continued it flourishes;

thus the sense is "practice makes a master." Again, periphrasis occurs when foulness is avoided by a circumlocution, as in Virgil:

> Lying on his spouse's lap he sought peaceful rest. [26]

Or this:

> Through gifts the adultress favors the adulterer;
>   Relying on a gift Venus gains hospitality within the
>   confines of shame.

In both examples, copulation is implied with becoming words.

---

[25] *Aen.* IV. 584-85.
[26] *Aen.* VIII. 406.

22. Change of the Active to the Passive. Further, there is another change of words and sentences, but one retains meanings by equivalence, when active constructions are dissolved into passive or vice versa, like this:

> Love tortures the gods, the gods are tortured by love;
> Fraud dissuades the boy, the boy is dissuaded by fraud.

Almost all transitive constructions can be converted in this manner.

—23. Moreover, another manner in which sentences and words are changed is when a simple or partial meaning is filled out by the use of phrases or clauses, or the converse, as if in the place of a partial meaning of this verb "he blushes" there is said "A blush reddens his face," or for "he mourns" one would say "He moistens his face with tears," or for "he becomes angry" one would say "Threatening anger leaps up." Many examples of this kind can be detected. Similarly, as serving for the supplementing of sentences, expressions within statements can be substituted.

24. The Exchange of Synonymous Words. The following concerns the exchange of words and not meaning where synonyms are most necessary. For synonyms possess the same meaning but from different viewpoints; hence the one can in most cases substitute for the other. Nor is the expression "in most cases" meaningless. For there are numerous synonyms which because of different connotations, do not participate in mutual usage, but still the meaning of one can be attributed to the meaning of the other; as in this example:

> Locks become hair; straits become the sea;
> Wind becomes a breeze; the crop, a harvest; the inn, a
>   home.

Indeed these nouns have varied connotations. Hence, one does not fill out the other except when authors improperly use them. **25.** Therefore, in this part the versifier should be experienced in the denotation and connotations of words, and from these two the function of a word is derived. **Ten Faults.** Ignorance of the meaning of words is productive of more harm than all of the other offenses of learning, which number ten, namely these: involvement in obscure brevity (whence Horace:

> Striving to be brief,
> I become obscure.) [27]

a digression in superfluous verbosity; the construction of pared discourse; the wandering of a bobbing mentality; craggy complications of meaning; unlimited confusion of discourse; sterility of untrained talent; the indecorous rattle of a headlong tongue; a mutilated confusion of words; ignor-

---

[27] *Ars Poet.* 25.

ance of the meaning of words. **26.** Hence to remedy such offences, we should especially emulate usage in a beautiful marriage of words,

> In his hand lies the decision, the right and the norm
>   of speech.

For usage is expressions that are "lackeys" and "tax-payers," and obey it as a father of the household. Hence, because its authority outweighs an analogy no one should presume to go beyond its liberty and permission, but words should be so properly placed that from their proper position the meter may seem to be at play more becomingly. —**27.** Further, a word can be the substitute for another if its meaning surpasses the meaning of the other, as in Statius:

> His death certain. Oenides, too proud to take plunder,
>   passes him by. [28]

"too proud," that is, "scornful," for pride comes before scorn. **28.** And likewise, when the meanings of words have mutual compatibility, as when Horace says "admire nothing." [29] that is, "desire nothing." **29.** Likewise, when what pertains to the subject is ascribed to a property, as in Lucan:

> All power
> Is impatient of a partner. [30]

"power," that is, "powerful person." **30.** Or, when what pertains to the thing caused is ascribed to the cause, as in Virgil:

> I remember myself spending long suns in song. [31]

that is, "days." For the sun is the efficient cause of day. **31.** Also, exchange of words is made in many other ways, as when words have a linking or related meaning, or when synodoche or metonymy is used.

32. Correction or Grammar. The following concerns correction. Correction, as here understood, is an examination of metrical rhythm which eliminates defects and furnishes an improvement for beauty; in it three things concern the pupil and two, the corrector; the latter are the marking of faults and indication of remedies. In these two procedures some planned order should be observed. **33.** For the marking of faults precedes their removal, then follows the improvement of beauty to be chosen.

---

[28] *Theb.* VII. 588.
[29] Cf. *Ep.* VI. 1.
[30] *Phars.* I. 93.
[31] *Ecl.* IX. 52.

Indeed, if the elimination of faults were not coming first, the improvement of beauty would be useless, according to what Horace says:

> Unless the vessel is uncontaminated, whatever you pour
> into it will turn sour.[32]

And although the judging of verses has been explained in many places above, some remaining points should be taken up. **34.** Indeed, in correction of verses we shall have to proceed clause by clause, separately, in conformity with zeugma or with hypozeusix. Indeed, never or rarely do I wish the meaning of verses to be given limits, unless the verse contain a general meaning; rather, let the meaning of the hexameter be extended to the pentameter, or let the phrases of the pentameter begin in the hexameter. Indeed, the hexameter and the pentameter have a companion and indivisible function. For a pentameter should be the servant or handmaid of the hexameter either by explaining its meaning or concluding it. For it is proper that things which share a function be companions in their purpose. **35.** However, not all defects in meter can always be corrected by the teacher, according to Ovid:

> It is not always in the physician's power to give relief
> to the sick.
> At times the ailment is stronger than disciplined art.[33]

Hence, because he who is not fit today will be less fit tomorrow, one must insist upon daily practice without any intervals lest the insolence of ignorance create harm, lest a little spark of sickness flare up into a conflagration. Indeed

> The medicine is prepared too late when the
> Evil has strengthened through long delays.[34]

36. Ovid testifies to the efficacy of practice saying:

> The drop hollows out a stone (only by falling often).[35]

Hence elsewhere Ovid says:

> Nothing is mightier than practice.[36]

And again:

> Experience is unlearned slowly.[37]

---

[32] *Ep.* I. 2. 54.
[33] *Pont.* I. 3. 17.
[34] *Rem.* 92-93.
[35] *Pont.* IV. 10. 5.
[36] *Ars.* II. 345.
[37] Rem. 503.

Although nature is the foundation of talent, usage develops it, and practice strengthens it, and perseverance crowns it. —**37.** Moreover, a transference of meaning to a third verse should not be made lest a boring hyperbaton be incurred.

38. Further, a monosyllabic word should never end a verse, lest, as we read in Horace, from a mountain rising in limitless size ultimately

> a ridiculous mouse is born.[38]

or lest a jar become a small pitcher. Whence in Horace:

> A jar began to form,
> Why, as the wheel turned, did it become a pitcher?[39]

39. The pentameter should always end in dissyllables, unless some urgent reason comes in the way. **40.** Also, a graceful recitation and the distinctiveness of clauses should be particularly observed. For very often the manner of reciting is more efficacious than the substance of the recitation,

> And because you recite poorly it is no longer yours.

41. There still remains much information concerning correction. But since judgments on verses have been discussed everywhere in the foregoing sections, we must hurry on to ensuing matters lest I seem to make the same currents go in circles. I also prefer that the diligent listener experience a live hearing, rather than a written work. As Horace attests:

> What finds entrance through the ear stirs the mind more
> Slowly than what is entrusted to the faithful eyes.[40]

42. There are some unlearned ones who usurp the office of correcting; and they, blind leading the blind, fall in a pit together, like Rufinus. But since in the kingdom of the blind, the king is a one-eyed man, and he has a people which trusts him; and they are perverted with the perverse, they redden with Rufus, and are made blind with the blind.

43. Points Which Pertain to the Student. There follows the three things which pertain to the student; they are these: admission of error, the avoidance of cover-up, and the submission to blame. The admission of error prompts forgiveness, avoidance of cover-up eludes arrogance, the submission to blame assures correction. Cover-up should be removed lest someone's fault be turned back on the innocent. For the guilt of the

---

[38] *Ars. Poet.* 139.
[39] *Ars. Poet.* 21.
[40] *Ars. Poet.* 180-81.

offender very often falls on the head of the innocent. And yet the fault will often be slight, if frequency be excluded. For

> If, as often as men err, Jupiter were to hurl his thunderbolt
> He would soon be weaponless.[41]

44. Those whose faults are daily and who need a bridle more than spurs ought to be rebuked very often, lest the instructors silence appear to be a substitute for yielding. For the impunity of the transgressor is the leader of transgression. On this matter the corrector must be vigilant. Ovid attests:

> This is a greater labor than writing.[42]

45. Further, what Horace says about the examination of verses should not be neglected, namely, the release of words from their metrical rule; and if considered as prose they are pleasing and have a beautiful bond, they will gain a far more pleasing position in meter. Thus Horace says in the *Satires,*

> Therefore it is not enough to write a verse in plain words;
> Were you to break it up, any father whatever would be
>   angered
> In the same manner as the actor in the play.[43]

46. Concerning Correction. There is still another lesson of Horace about correction in the second book of the *Epistles,* speaking in this vein:

> But he who will desire to have composed a poem true to
>   the laws,
> With his tablets he will assume the spirit of a conscientious
>   censor;
> He will be courageous to expel from their place whatever
>   words have too little lustre,
> Or are without weight, or considered unworthy of respect,
> No matter how reluctantly they are removed.[44]

And further on he says:

> He will pour out his treasures and bless Latium with a
>   rich speech:
> He will prune excessive growth: he will smooth the too rough
>   by judicious care:
> He will change what lacks vigor.[45]

---

[41] Ovid, *Tristia,* II. 1. 33-34.

[42] *Pont.* I. 5. 17.

[43] *Sat.* I. IV. 54.

[44] *Ep.* II. 2. 109-13.

[45] *Ep.* II. 2. 121-23.

47. Again, after excepting those of like style, because the wickedness of Rufus' style overflows in him more fully and will perhaps arise in his successor, whatever has been said of Rufus and Rufinus is to be understood as spiritually applying to Arnulf of holy Evurcius; in my absence he irritates me with daily insult and his tongue, I think, is poisoned with the venom of envy. But whatever you presume to caw about me, Rufinus, "No dignity will make you worthy of Caesar's wrath." But it is difficult to kick against the goad; indeed, he who kicks strenuously against the goad irritates himself, victim of a double irritation. **48.** For, although I do so somewhat sparingly in this little work, yet in an exchange of epistles I will deliver a recompense you more fully deserve,

> And may you consider nothing to be safer in my life
>   Than verse under my guide.

Indeed, may my tongue not be considered slanderous if it slander a slanderer. I concur with Solomon when he says: "Answer a fool according to his folly, lest you be made like him." [46] Therefore, provoked by him

> I bite the biter; when oppressed, I oppress,
>   I injur when injured; it is fitting to balance out
>   retaliation with retaliation.

so that his wickedness, as I divide the memorial, can by no means be buried in the ashes of oblivion: [47]

> It is shameful to Rufus that I publish his ruddy deceits;
>   But still, unwillingly I shall be his ruin.
> Burst, Rufus, I intend to speak, so Rufus' sides may burst.
>   Whatever I shall attempt to say will be in verse.
> You tremble with the onset of amazement when you alone
>   Are loving Thais, you alone; nor do you have her,
>   but only think so.
> The ruddy bond colors both alike, they rufinize,
>   Rufa lies under Rufus, the she-ape under the he-ape, the
>   she-goat under the he-goat.
> Invidious Rufus, with good fingers stretched for interest,
>   You contrive against the laws of Otho and favor the
>   drunkard's wall.

49. The Conclusion. Because we have spoken about the two ways of beginning material, namely through zeugma and ypozeuxis, and about proceeding with a general sententia or proverb, and about maintaining the unity of measure, the manner of writing, the attributes of action and of persons, the tripartite refinement of versifying, about figures and tropes, the handling of the material, the exchange, and correction; a discussion of conclusion follows so that the present work my happily be concluded in its

---

[46] Cf. *Proverbs* XXVI. 4; which reads "Do *not* answer a fool. . . ."

[47] Sedgwick notes that the following verses are "a jumble of parodies" taken from Ovid, Virgil and Horace and adjusted to form this climactic attack on Arnulf (Rufus).

conclusion. Conclusion, as is understood here, is the termination according to the rules of meter and involving uniformity of the subject-matter. **50.** Variety in conclusion abounds in the authors. It comes about by the epilogue, that is, through a recapitulation of the meaning, as in the first narrative of Avianus, where it says:

> Whoever believes faithfulness is a feminine trait, let him
> know
> These words are directed to him, and that he himself is
> indicated by this art.[48]

Another conclusion is made by emending the work, as in the *Thebiad* of Statius:

> [envy] shall pass away, and after my death your well-
> deserved honors will be paid.[49]

Again, very often a conclusion can be made by a plea for indulgence; hence in Ovid:

> I was on the point of making corrections, had it been
> allowed.[50]

Or it can be made by a demonstration of pride, as in the book on *The Remedies of Love:*

> After me, you, men and women, soothed by my songs,
> Will offer pious vows to the holy poet.[51]

An anticipated conclusion is very often made by authors whose death is expected before the conclusion, which should be called a termination rather than a conclusion, as in Lucan:

> After the walls were shatteered, Magnus, trampling on the
> ramparts, was surrounded.[52]

A conclusion can be made, too, by an expression of thanks, as in the *Bucolics:*

> Here will be sufficient, O Muses, for your poet to have sung.

Virgil seems to show thanks to the Muses by saying "your." **51.** Similarly, a conclusion is to be made when the present work is terminated with the praise of God; from his fount the stream of this present work has flowed; for this work I am his legate, and his legatee I desire to be; whatever charm may have crept in here he has deigned that it be assigned to those of lesser age through the medium of my teaching.

---

[48] *Fable,* I. 16-17.

[49] *Theb.* XII. 819.

[50] *Tristia,* I. 7. 40.

[51] *Rem.* 813-14.

[52] *Phars.* X. 546.

O Christ, to you be honor, to you be praise who reigns
      with the Father,
  King with king, God with God forever.
Other in being from the Father, yet nothing else but what the
      Father would be,
    Indeed, not the same person as the Father, yet the same as
      the Father.
Father, Son, Spirit, all are God, one being not one person,
  Three persons, not three beings. Triune and the same.
Otherness does not divide what is united by nature,
    And there is one completeness in three; the triune union
      amazes us.
As vessel I give thanks to the potter, as fabric to the craftsman,
    As servant to the king, creature to the creator,
      child to the father;
As he dictates, I speak; as he guides, I cruise;
    As he leads, I am led; in him the most radiant harbor
      I take my joy.
Wisdom knows not how to savor him, nor report proclaim him.
    Nor mind can tell of him, nor tongue speak of him, nor
      place contain him.
He is good without quality and immense without quantity,
    He renders false the notions expressed by voice.
He is day without cloud, all things in all,
    Entire without parts, powerful without condition.
Whom discernment cannot discern, since in ignorance it
      does not know
    How to know; and him words fear to name.
Space is amazed that he is greater, time that he antedates time,
    End that he is the end, origin that he is the progenitor.
He the unmoved moves all things, he triune and one,
    Is three, is one, to the three there may be one honor.
Him the eye perceives not, the ear captures not,
    Him reason knows not: let nurturing faith make whole.

A Parisian. I hasten my steps; Sweet patron of mine
  In the time of Primas, Orleans, farwell.
This little sum has instructed the young in versifying,
    the name
    Is taken from the material: it can teach the highest things.
Live, I pray, and do not dread the mouthing of spite,
  Little treatise, put into form during two months.
These things I remember, it delights to remember; the
      meadows have drunk an abundance.
    Here ends the completed work of Matthew of Vendome.

And if anything remains, let it be burned to ashes, that is, let it be entrusted
to the Holy Spirit. Amen.